ONCE UPON A TIME

ONCE UPON A TIME

A Storytelling Handbook

Lucille N. Breneman

and Bren Breneman

Nelson-Hall nh Chicago

Library of Congress Cataloging in Publication Data

Breneman, Lucille N.
 Once upon a time.

 Bibliography: p.
 Includes index.
 1. Story-telling. I. Breneman, Bren. II. Title.
 LB1042.B67   1983   372.6'4   83-10990
 ISBN 0-8304-1007-4

Manufactured in the United States of America

10   9   8   7   6   5   4   3   2   1

The paper in this book is pH neutral (acid-free).

*To our students
who inspired us to write this book*

No, it'll not do just to read the
old tales out of a book. You've
got to tell 'em to make 'em go right.

— Richard Chase, *Grandfather Tales*

Contents

Acknowledgments

THANKS TO MANY COLLEAGUES for their encouragement, but particularly three—Mavis B. Ferguson, Donald W. Klopf, and Wayne H. Oxford; to Bret Breneman for his advice and editing of the final script; to the instructors who have tested *Once Upon a Time* by using the material set forth here in their storytelling classes; to Mary Breneman for the illustrations; to the patient secretaries, Velma Joy Francisco and Laura Tomoyasu, Speech Department, University of Hawaii; to the Nelson-Hall editors.

Introduction

For three attempts at telling stories the boy did nothing but stand in front of the class and relate story incidents, unemotionally and totally uninvolved. No progress was evident nor did it look as though there ever would be. A conference was held with him, highlighting his need to work on characterization, visualization, and bodily movements. Practice sessions, emphasizing these areas for the next story, were held with the instructor — seemingly with little progress. The instructor will never forget how discouraged he was following the student's last session.

But something marvelous happened between that session and the boy's telling of the story for the class. From the moment he appeared and spoke his first words, the story began to unfold. He was telling a children's story, and although his listeners were adults they were immediately transplanted to a child's storyland. The boy was totally involved with the telling. No longer was he just relating incidents — he was personally reliving them. He had entered the never-never land and taken us with him.

IT IS SAID OPPORTUNITIES do not come to those who wait; they are captured by those who attack. We all want recognition, and this desire to be accepted is natural and worthy. Storytelling will not open the halls of public acclaim for everyone, but it does just that for many on the school campus and in more sophisticated areas of adult life as well. It can be an invaluable tool in the life's work of any man or woman.

There are many opportunities on the campus and beyond to tell stories. Remember, opportunity is what the wise man sees and makes the most of. Small social groups need entertainers; variety show producers are on the alert for acts. Community organizations, both social and service, are always looking for talent. Become interested in storytelling; determine to use your personality as the storytelling medium and you may gain that recognition which we all need.

A study of the techniques of storytelling is valuable not only for the art itself but as an aid in many professions. Most public speakers tell stories to establish rapport, illustrate points, create mood, build climaxes, and for other purposes. Every elementary teacher should be an effective storyteller, and teachers at all levels will find the skill an asset in teaching. The librarian who can stimulate an appreciation of literature by telling stories is to be sought after. Nurses have many opportunities to tell stories.

Skill in storytelling is an asset in most professions and is at the heart of some. Many of the techniques used by the comedian and the actor are necessary for effective storytelling. Most comedians and masters of ceremonies use storytelling techniques in their individual acts. In addition these people establish certain unique personality traits that appeal to their audiences. If you aspire to become a professional entertainer, use every opportunity to tell stories. There is no speech activity that provides more incentive for intimate communication and control of empathic and emotional responses of the listeners. If you have the personal drive and incentive to become a professional entertainer, storytelling may very well be your springboard.

People have always liked to tell stories and sing songs, and they have always liked to listen to them. This is the way of folklore. Wherever people were mingling in almost any situation — work or social — a storyteller found receptive ears. Some members of the audience would try to memorize a story that had special appeal to them as it was told. Later, when they were in groups they would tell the story as they remembered it. Each telling of the story differed somewhat. In fact the story changed many times in the telling. The original teller of the tale was soon forgotten and the story became a story of the folk — called "lore of the folk" or "folklore."

People in every part of the world have told stories. Folklore attests to the fact that, throughout history, the experiences, reactions, and feelings of people everywhere have been similar. Here is a glimpse of the Irish tradition of storytelling.

The Gaelic people have a long heritage in the art of storytelling. The raconteurs of medieval times must have attained a high degree of artistry. Their imaginative tales enliven the pages of Irish and Scottish history and represent some of the world's best heroic literature and folklore.

Both aristocratic and plebian raconteurs in Ireland cultivated their art through successive generations. Their sagas have been carefully copied on vellum which is treasured as a tangible record. A few folklorists, since the middle of the Nineteenth Century, have recorded stories told orally by the humble taleweavers. These stories were narrated by the common people of Ireland in their cottages for hundreds of years.

In tucked away places in Ireland where Gaelic is still the favorite language, old men and women continue the oral

tradition of storytelling. Displaying fantastic memories, these vanishing people — the intelligent, illiterate, backwoods storytellers — can tell two or three hundred stories at the drop of a hat. Many of them are members of families which have nurtured storytellers for four or more generations. Some of these modern reciters of Irish hero or wonder tales may be the lineal descendants of the storytellers of a thousand years ago. They learned their stories by hearing them. Many of the stories were handed on by word of mouth by one family since the Seventeenth Century. These raconteurs may bridge the gap between centuries. By their art, they may picture the nameless storytellers and creators of the heroic medieval literature of Ireland.[1]

It is not our purpose here to trace the long and colorful history of storytelling, because its roots stretch back over thousands of years to the beginning of man's communicating experiences in the simplest narrative. We should point out, however, that long before there were written records, in the early stages of humanity's development, the storyteller performed an important function for society in reporting news, sharing experiences, teaching, and transmitting ideas and values from one generation to another. Storytelling developed also as a great entertainment medium, consequently becoming an art form.

Although storytelling has continuously served society in these functions, its role and its significance has fluctuated from one period to another. With the widespread use of newspapers, radio, and TV, the storyteller's role as the major means of imparting information and preserving records diminished. However, at present there are still a few Eastern countries (where great majorities of people are illiterate) that depend on

---

[1]Bren Breneman and Lucille Breneman, "Once Upon a Time," *The Speech Teacher,* 4 (Sept. 1965):216–23.

professional storytellers as a major source for imparting information and instructing the masses directly. But worldwide it is for the other functions that storytelling is most important.

Today there is a resurgence of interest in the art of storytelling, and in folklore. For many years, a few concerned folklorists throughout the modern world have been collecting folktales and folksongs, stories of the people that originated and were passed on by word of mouth only. There also has developed recently among some cultures a desire to learn more about modern society's beginnings and development, and the folklore collections are a rich source for this purpose. Storytelling is recognized with a renewed fervor as a means of building pride in one's own culture. It is recognized by a growing number of people as a significant means of sharing experiences, teaching, and entertaining.

In the last half-dozen years there has been a noticeable increase of interest and activity in the art of storytelling. Scattered throughout the United States and Canada are storytelling organizations and centers that have developed and grown. These organizations sponsor festivals, conferences, and workshops in storytelling. Many of them send out newsletters and journals to their members. The leading story center is called NAPPS — National Association for the Preservation and Perpetuation of Storytelling — located in Jonesboro, Tennessee. The NAPPS staff puts out a monthly publication called *The Yarnspinner*. They also publish an up-to-date directory of professional storytellers throughout the United States.

More than a hundred professional storytellers are making a living in the United States by telling stories at universities, service clubs, libraries, festivals, and workshops. NAPPS sponsors numerous conferences and workshops during the year, its annual storytelling festival drawing some fifteen hundred people.

NAPPS is not the only site of activity. The national calendar announces some twenty-five conferences or festivals of two to four days in length, scheduled from New York to California over a three-month period. There is truly a revival of interest in the art of storytelling.

Storytelling is an interpretative art falling under the area of aesthetic communication, more often called oral interpretation. Storytelling differs somewhat from other interpretative arts in story material, presentation, and preparation. The storyteller's material is restricted to the narrative form — to the recounting of either real or imaginary events. Most storytellers use the extemporaneous delivery in presentation. They have spent many hours in preparation — if their storytelling is effective — but they have not memorized the author's words. They have analyzed the story thoughtfully, edited and adapted it for telling, and then have told the story again and again to an imaginary audience, using their own sentence structure until they have command of fluency. While achieving fluency, they concentrate on directness with an imaginary audience, recognizing that storytelling requires a more intimate communication than almost any other interpretative art. They work with verbal and nonverbal techniques. They listen to their voices attentively, trying to develop a flexibility that creates mood and suspense, voice quality that suggests character, and all of the vocal techniques that will help the audience to recognize story progression — transition, rising action, and climax. They work for expressiveness and control of nonverbal elements, attempting to keep eyes, face, and body alive to all of the mental images they wish to share with the audience.

What is storytelling? What do we want from the storyteller? Storytelling is the seemingly easy, spontaneous, intimate sharing of a narrative with one or many persons; the storyteller relates, pictures, imagines, builds what happens, and suggests characters, involving him- or herself and listeners in the total story — all manifested through voice and body.

The fact that success in storytelling does not require beauty or glamour should encourage all of us. Personal size, lines, or form seem to be unimportant in determining the success of a storyteller. Use what you have, what you are as the interpretative medium, forgetting self in your spirited intent to project storyland to your audience, and that self will become an effective communicative instrument.

There are many ways of learning how to tell a story. We have known many superior storytellers who never had formal training in the art of storytelling. One of our close relatives was such a storyteller. We have spent many pleasant hours with him. He was a stimulating conversationalist and seemed always to have a story to highlight a point. We have heard him tell dozens of stories and anecdotes and seldom did we hear the same story. His purpose for relating a yarn was always a pure love for the story and intent to share it. Many is the time when we have seen him so caught up with the humor of the story that he laughed so hard in the telling of it that tears rolled down his cheeks. His reactions were totally spontaneous and therefore captivating and infectious.

Perhaps you may be inclined to call our relative a natural storyteller. You may go on to say that you have known many natural storytellers, and that you feel that storytelling is a special gift — that "some have it, some don't!" There may be a few "natural" storytellers, but most of them only *seem* to be able to artfully entertain without any effort. We are dealing with an acquired skill, and any storyteller who is able to entertain many different audiences, in many different situations, with a large repertoire of stories has worked at the craft. He or she has learned, though not all learning was necessarily the result of conscious effort. Many of the great storytellers of the past studied their art in a disciplined fashion as apprentices — long before more formal training was available. A traditional Irish storyteller on the rocky coast of Connemara, Ireland, told us how he practiced his art. Sitting in a pub this teller of tales entertained us for two hours. Afterwards we asked him many questions. One question was, "How did you learn your stories?" His answer, "I used to walk behind my father as he followed the mule and plow. While plowing my father would practice telling his stories almost constantly, becoming so involved at times that he forgot he was plowing." All effective storytellers have practiced their art.

Some individuals have more aptitude, or talent, for story-telling or any other art than do others. We have been surprised, however, at the large number of students in our classes who have been unaware of their own abilities. Most encouraging of all are the indications that anyone who wants to can become a good storyteller. Of the hundreds of students who have entered our classes over the years, there has never been one student who really worked assiduously with intent to succeed who did not become an interesting storyteller. We could give you many examples of students who at first seemingly had every reason for failure — but who became excellent storytellers. Two immediately come to mind.

The first case was a girl who was so shy in front of an audience she couldn't project her name sufficiently to be heard in the front row. The girl was extremely fearful of any speaking situation, but she was an excellent dancer who had studied ballet since childhood and appeared in many dance recitals without undue fear of an audience. Although fearful when entering the storytelling class, she had something in her favor — a determination to succeed. She told her first story to the instructor privately. She was very nervous but did manage to get through her entire story. In telling her second story to the class, she was doing nothing other than saying words very softly — but again she was successful in getting through the story. With the telling of the third story there was a noticeable improvement, so much so that members of the class became excited. As she finished, loud applause echoed and re-echoed in the classroom. From then on her progress in storytelling was almost unbelievable. By the end of the semester she was the most skillful storyteller in that class. We shall always remember her as one of the most entertaining storytellers it has been our pleasure to hear.

The second image from the past is of the boy whose story is told at the beginning of this introduction. For three tellings of stories he seemed to make no progress; he only related incidents in monotone. After sessions with the instructor, highlighting his need to work in certain areas, there still seemed to be little improvement.

But something marvelous happened between that session and his telling of the story for the class. From the moment he appeared and started with his first words, the story began to unfold. He was telling a children's story, and although his listeners were adults we were immediately transplanted to a child's storyland. The boy was totally involved with the telling. No longer was he just relating incidents, he was personally living them. He had entered the never-never land and taken us with him.

Storytelling is for anyone who wants to share stories. It is for you. Storytellers are different, just as individuals are different, and they should remain so, developing skills that contribute to their effectiveness in storytelling.

The varied experiences gained in telling stories to many groups is of inestimable value in all speech training. You can read in a textbook that every speaking situation is different, but only by facing numerous audiences will you realize this truth and experience the challenges of different audience situations. One successful experience is father to other successes. As the French statesman and diplomat Talleyrand said, "Nothing succeeds so well as success." Use all of the opportunities offered to tell your story and you will develop a background of experience that will help you in any speaking situation.

You may be fearful of strange audiences at first, but if you prevail you will find each experience easier — like the little city girl who was spending her first summer in the country. She was asked how she liked running about barefoot. "At first I could hardly walk," she said, "but the rocks got softer every day." Facing an audience will become easier and, finally, exhilarating.

Certain techniques for each speech activity should be learned. Knowledge of these is imperative if you wish to make progress in the communicative skills. All growth in skill, however, depends upon activity. There is no development without effort. You must practice to develop any skill. If you wish to play the piano, you practice the piano. If you wish to become a figure skater, you put on skates every chance you get. If you wish to become a skillful storyteller, you practice alone and in front of audiences.

Once upon a Time: A Storytelling Handbook presents a systematic approach for developing skills in storytelling.

In the first half of the book, we describe the procedures and principles involved in choosing a story; analyzing and adapting the story; working for fluency, characterization, visualization, bodily action and control; unity and polish; and anticipating a real audience. This embodies the main thrust of the book — presenting principles and techniques that may be applied to *all* storytelling.

Next, we single out biography from other types of stories based on fact, such as true experiences and great historical events. If you are a student and are limited to one factual story, as most students are in a one-semester course, we suggest that the experience be in story biography. Selected principles from concentrated study here may also be applied to other factual story types. The nature of story biography, choice of subject, structure, and presentation are discussed.

The next part, Selected Samples, includes sample stories based on biography, story biography analysis papers, a few selected stories, and an original story.

The last part is an annotated bibliography that includes fables, fairy tales, folktales, legends, fantasies, and children's stories for storytelling; short stories for storytelling; and short stories and novels for interpretative reading and storytelling.

CHAPTER ONE

Choosing a Story

THE STORYTELLER'S REALM OF material is wide, drawing from the real and imaginary, the old and the new. You may choose from the broad area of folklore, or you may choose a short story, an episode from a novel, a true experience, or biography. We urge you to make your first selection from folklore. The folktales, legends, myths, fairy tales, epics, fables, parables, and ballads are all story forms leading back to the beginning of civilization. Many of these stories originated in the telling and were handed down by word of mouth.

Some of the first recorded stories, around six thousand years ago, were told by sons of Cheops, the pharaoh known as the pyramid builder. This ruler must have been gifted with highly imaginative children. It is said that each son entertained his father on a certain night with an old tale. Each son attempted to tell a more interesting tale than his brothers before him. Thousands of years later, this device of a group of stories suspended on a central framework was used in the *1001 Tales of the Arabian Nights* and still later in Chaucer's *Canterbury Tales.* [1]

Historical records exist of storytellers in many countries of ancient times; however, we are most aware of European storytellers in what we call the Middle Ages. Thousands of storytellers lived in the British Isles and Europe during that time. A tale is told of one royal occasion, the wedding of Margaret of England in 1209. It is said that 426 minstrels were employed to entertain with story. [2] Evidently her father, the king, enjoyed entertainment.

If there were thousands of storytellers in the Middle Ages it seems reasonable that a host of storytellers must have preceded them, and many have followed — all of these people telling tales, sharing their imaginations, emotions, experiences, sorrows, stories of common people, tales of heroes, insights of the infinite, and intimate yarns of animals.

As these tales and experiences were told, and as people began wondering about themselves different forms of stories began to take shape. Myriad storytellers trod the world's paths, telling stories in humble cottages and in castles of the rich and powerful. Folktales, myths, legends, fairy tales, fables, parables, epics, and ballads evolved as the storytellers travelled.

Many similarities exist among the story forms in folklore, and some scholars use the terms "folktale" and "fairy tale" interchangeably. The following description of the story forms may be of some help as you begin your search for a story.

Folktales spring from the way of life of any culture. They are the stories of the common folk growing out of their needs to express themselves. These tales were told by word of mouth

---

[1] Ruth Tooze, *Storytelling* (Englewood Cliffs, N.J.: 1959). p. 14.
[2] Joan I. Glazer and William Gurney III, *Introduction to Children's Literature* (New York: McGraw-Hill Book Co., 1979).

and handed down from one generation to the next. Many have been collected and retold by writers and editors. You will want to have folktales in your repertoire; they are an excellent source for your first selection.

People have always liked to tell stories about heroes and their great adventures. Hero tales probably began as stories about a real person and happening. As the stories were told over and over and passed from one generation to another the hero became bigger and the happening more fantastic until the stories became legends. How much fact and how much fantasy there is in a legend, nobody knows, but you will find them great for storytelling. Take a look at the Paul Bunyan and John Henry stories.

Some of the hero tales developed into long epics such as the *Odyssey.* Epics are narratives of heroes who play some very

important role in the lives of humans and whose activities often seem to be carefully watched, guided, and protected by divine power. A grandeur and unusual power dignify this story. While full epics usually are too long for storytelling, you may find episodes within the epics are suitable.

Myths deal with gods shaped in the image of man. They are influenced by humanity's questioning of the mysteries of life and the infinite. All peoples have their myths. Among the best known throughout the world are the myths of Greek gods — Zeus, Apollo, and others. Myths are fine for storytelling, although many will require cutting.

The fairy tale is highly imaginative, usually one author's original creation; for example, Hans Christian Andersen's "Ugly Duckling" and "The Emperor's New Clothes." Rare powers and magic play a big part in the weaving of a fairy tale. Little people, such as pixies, dwarfs, goblins, leprechauns, trolls, elves, gnomes, brownies, and menehunes are often major folk in these stories. If these "little people" appeal to you, then fairy tales should be fun to tell.

Stories using animals to point out a lesson are called fables. From the beginning, animals have been very important to humans as pets, as beasts of burden, and as food. They became a part of various stories. At some point, these animal stories began to teach a lesson. A moral or simple truth was summarized in one sentence at the end of each story. Aesop's fables, which date back to the seventh century B.C., are perhaps the best known of all fables. These fables are very short; therefore, one could put several of them together for a five- to six-minute presentation.

A parable is a short fictitious story which deals with some religious principle or projects a moral attitude. Probably the best examples are to be found in the Bible — for instance, "The Good Samaritan."

A ballad tells a story. It is set in metrical form and usually concerns love and some bold adventure. Folksongs and folk stories developed together. The old storytellers often mixed the arts of music, dance, and storytelling. For your first story, we suggest that you not choose a ballad because it would require memorizing the story word for word.

Each story choice should be influenced by the purpose of the story, the occasion on which it is to be told, the setting, and the audience. As a student, your general purpose would be to tell stories in order to develop your skill in the art of story-telling. Your immediate audience would be your classmates.

Although we suggest that you make your first selection from folklore, ultimately you will want experiences in as many of the different kinds of stories as possible. Whether you choose a legend, folktale, fairy tale, or short story, there are certain elements that make some stories better for telling than others.

CRITERIA FOR SELECTION

Personal Appreciation of the Story

Does the story appeal to you? In a quick reading of or listening to the story, does it capture your attention and involve you in what is happening? You must like a story if you expect to cause others to like it. Your first impression is important. The spontaneous reaction of pleasure or excitement you get from a story without analyzing why you got it is a significant factor in personal appreciation.

If the story appeals to you, then ask yourself if you want to work with it and if you feel capable at this stage in your train-ing to share it with others. If in a second reading, the plot seems rather complex, or if there are more important characters than you think you can handle, or if much of the charm of the story depends on the language as it is written, then perhaps you should note this story for future telling, after you have gained some experience.

Nothing is more important in choosing a story than your personal appreciation of it.

One Major Plot

The story you choose should have one central plot, uncluttered with secondary plots. The audience cannot go back and reread a part of the story if they have become confused about what is happening. At the same time if the major plot is strong and not dependent on secondary plots for wholeness, then you may drop complicating secondary plots. The story should have an easy-to-follow plot after preparation for telling.

Colorful Characters

Are the characters interesting, believable, and fun to work with? Are there enough contrasts among the characters for you to be able to portray them or at least give suggestions of differing characteristics? Although there is no ideal number of characters to a story, the storyteller is wise to keep the major characters to a small number.

Not all characters need be people. Often, as in fables, there are animals endowed with human characteristics and abilities. Brer Fox and Brer Rabbit, for example, are intriguing characters. Don't avoid stories with animals.

Action and Suspense

Select a story filled with action — with one suspenseful event building on another to the climax — and half the battle of holding your audience's attention will be won. The exception here is in choosing a story for the very young. Suspense stories may be disturbing — that is, too exciting — for very young children. They will respond more favorably to repeated jingles, phrases, sounds, rhythm, movement, and the cumulative patterns. They love to join the storyteller in refrains and to supply words in repeated patterns. Except for the very young, however, most children (and adults) respond favorably to action and suspense in a story.

An Arresting Introduction

The introduction here does not refer to the introductory remarks of the storyteller, but rather to the opening of a story as set down by an author or editor. This introduction generally lays forth the setting and time of the story and introduces the person or persons principally involved. The introduction should be short and have a minimum of descriptive passages and of antecedent action.

The storyteller wants to arrest the attention of his audience by quickly creating the world of his story and then moving on to the happenings. Many of the old folktales take care of the opening in one sentence. "The Peddler and His Caps," for example, starts "Once upon a time there was a peddler who sold caps." Two additional statements give us a little more information about the peddler and the way he carries his caps, and we are right into the story.

Long descriptive passages, though they may be beautiful, tend to impede progress, especially at the beginning. The same is true in the relating of much antecedent action — that is, telling of things that occurred in the past before you can get on with the "now" happenings of the story. This is not to say that you should avoid the use of description and antecedent action completely, but rather that in most instances, they should be used sparingly.

Obviously you should not reject a story because the introduction does not measure up to the rest of the story. Consider whether it is possible to alter the introduction and thus improve it from the viewpoint of the storyteller.

Appropriateness of Language and Style in Writing

The choice of words should be true to the nature of the story. Probably little needs to be said under this topic, because whether you realize it or not when you first read a story your appreciation and interest, or lack of it, is greatly influenced by the writer's style. This is true whether he or she is the original author or the reteller of the tale. One of the strong appeals of Richard Chase's collections of folktales (for example, *Grandfather Tales*) is that he has captured in his written style a quality of folksy, spoken language. Even though as the storyteller you will use much of your own language, that language should be influenced by the style of the author, and it must be appropriate to the story and its characters.

Variety of Sensory Images

We so often think of seeing and hearing as the major components of our sensory world that we sometimes overlook touch, smell, taste, temperature, and motion. Most of the senses are important to a story and should be equally so for the storyteller. Look for the sensory images the writer has been able to produce with words. When you read, "He felt the plush warm velvet," can you experience touching velvet with your fingers? You must create that feeling for your listener. The storyteller has not only words with which to create sensory images but also his or her entire being. More will be said about the storyteller and sensory images under the "visualization" step of preparation, presented later in this book. At this point you are asked to be aware of the sensory images in the written story and to seek stories to tell with a variety of such images.

Length of Story

While the length of time available for telling a story depends on the occasion, for class purposes it should be five to ten minutes. Most stories from folklore are more effective if kept within the five- to seven-minute range, and some may be given satisfactory treatment in less than five minutes. Most short stories tend to take a little longer than folktales; therefore, we suggest a maximum of ten minutes for the telling of a short story. Students often think they need more than ten minutes to do justice to a story based on biography, but many have given beautiful, well-rounded story-biographies in eight minutes.

Let's say you are to appear on a program and have been given a time limit by the program manager, or you have imposed a limit on yourself. You must consider the length of the story and the possibility of cutting without detracting from the total effectiveness of the story.

Remember that the "telling" time and "reading" time are often not the same. Usually it takes less time to tell a story than it takes to read it aloud as the author wrote it. Most often you will tell the story in your own language rather than in that of the author's, and you may drop long descriptive passages and minor incidents in the telling. More will be said later about story editing and the options of the storyteller. It is sufficient here for you to recognize the potential a story has for editing, since that potential is as important as actual length in choosing a story.

Appropriateness for Your Audience

Since you will spend much time preparing the story you choose, it should be appropriate not only for a particular audience but for several others as well.

Perhaps you are a teacher or prospective teacher and you know you will be teaching fifth grade students in a certain school. Keep them in mind when choosing a story. Also consider other groups of children, such as boy scouts, girl scouts, summer recreation groups, and library audiences, for whom the story would be appropriate.

Not every story will meet all the nine criteria just discussed. Nevertheless, keep them in mind as you search for the story you want to tell. When you find one that ranks high in several criteria, select it, knowing that as you make the story yours for telling, you may be able to alter it to your satisfaction.

WHERE TO LOOK

With a wealth of story material available in collections of short stories, folktales, fairy tales, and legends in libraries, bookstores, schools, and at home, you might think that choosing one is no problem. The experiences of storytellers prove otherwise. In looking for a story, it is not simply a matter of reading and then thinking, "That's an interesting story; I like it." Story selection has to become more personal; it's got to be a particular story — "*the* story for me" — and that is not easy to find. Think of the process of choosing the story as an enriching experience in itself, a process through which you will become acquainted with many stories.

As you start your exploration, consider first your own resources. Think of the stories you have heard or read that made an impression on you. Look in your own library and talk to your family and friends about stories.

Second, consult annotated bibliographies, which should give you enough about a story so that you can decide whether you should read it. We recommend Ruth Tooze's *Storytelling,* particularly chapters "The Heritage" and "What Makes a Story Good to Tell," and the annotated bibliography.

Third, read, read, read, from any source that interests you and choose a story based on the criteria discussed previously. Again, let the first one come from the broad field of folklore. The story may be an old favorite, but it should be one that you have not previously worked on.

SUGGESTIONS FOR STORY SOURCES

You should not feel bound by someone else's "favorite list of stories," yet for getting started, you might find helpful the annotated bibliography at the end of this book. A few of the sources are listed here:

Arbuthnot, May Hill. *The Arbuthnot Anthology of Children's Literature.* Glenview, Ill.: Scott, Foresman, 1971. Part two, "Time for Magic: Old and New," contains folktales, fables, myths, epics, and modern fantasy.

Chase, Richard, ed. *Grandfather Tales: American-English Folk Tales.* Boston: Houghton Mifflin, 1948. Retelling of old English tales, influenced by a North Carolina setting.

Fitzgerald, Berdette S. *World Tales for Creative Dramatics and Storytelling.* Englewood Cliffs, N.J.: Prentice-Hall, 1962. An anthology of world folktales especially chosen for children. Over a hundred tales told simply, with little alteration.

Kaye, Danny, ed. *Around the World Story Book.* New York: Random House, 1960. A collection of 104 favorite stories, legends, fairy tales, and fables of people everywhere, past and present.

Sakado, Florence, ed. *Japanese Children's Favorite Stories.* 2d ed. Tokyo and Rutland, Vt.: Charles E. Tuttle, 1959. Twenty favorite stories — a delight for children in any land — beautifully illustrated.

Sawyer, Ruth. *The Way of the Storyteller.* New York: Viking Press, 1942. A book about storytelling, with many stories included.

Shedlock, Marie. *The Art of Storytelling.* New York: D. Appleton, 1951. A book about storytelling, with many stories included.

Tooze, Ruth. *Storytelling.* Englewood Cliffs, N.J.: Prentice-Hall, 1959. This book includes an extensive bibliography, much of which is annotated.

Velarde, Pablita. *Old Father the Storyteller.* Globe, Ariz.: Dale Stuart King, 1960. American Indian legends told and illustrated by the most noted Indian woman painter in the United States.

Warren, Robert Penn, and Erskine, Albert, eds. *Short Story Masterpieces.* New York: Dell, 1954. Thirty-six of the best stories of our time in an anthology ranging from the humor of James Thurber and Ring Lardner to the irony of Hemingway and Joyce.

CHAPTER TWO

Analyzing and Adapting the Story

IN THE PROCESS OF choosing the story, you will become familiar with it, particularly from the standpoint of the total effect or the unified whole. For a more thorough study of it, you should break the story into its parts and then put it back together in the way you plan to tell it.

ANALYSIS

Read the story carefully, taking particular note of the mood, theme, setting, plot, and characters. All of these elements are important in a story, but the dominance of one or the other differs according to an author's purpose. In many stories, plot is dominant; in some, character is the most important element. Mood is dominant in others. Or, plot and character may be equally balanced. Since you should emphasize the appropriate element or elements of the story in your telling, attention should be given to them at this stage of preparation.

What is the dominant mood? Does the story give you an overall sense of sadness, foreboding, mystery, happiness, pen-

25

siveness, fancifulness? Whatever the overall mood is, you will need to reflect it as you tell the story.

What is the theme of the tale? What does it say? Try to frame the theme in one statement. This may be some universal truth, such as, "Love conquers all," but theme may not necessarily be a moral maxim. In the story, "The Peddler and His Caps," the action centers around a peddler trying to retrieve his caps from monkeys who prankishly imitate all of his actions as he pleads and yells at them to return his caps. We have stated the theme for this folktale as, "Monkeys will be monkeys." As a part of a storytelling project carried on in several schools, this story was told to a fifth-grade class. Following the telling the students were asked how they would state the theme of the folktale. One bright-eyed boy spontaneously answered, "Monkeys see, monkeys do!" That fits perfectly. Neither the boy's statement of the theme nor our own projects a moral.

Since the theme of the story represents the author's message, you need to be aware of the theme; but in telling the story let the story itself carry the message through character and plot, without commenting on or referring to the theme as such. Particularly, following the conclusion of a story, avoid pointing out a moral.

This is not meant to suggest that stories that teach a lesson should be avoided. On the contrary, the lesson of a story may have a stronger impact on the audience if allowed to stand on its own in the context of the story. Recognize, however, that a few stories emphatically state the moral or theme. For example, James Thurber's fables typically end with "The moral of this story is. . . ." That tag is a part of the story, and contributes significantly to the humor and appeal of Thurber's fables. Therefore, if you were telling a Thurber fable or any other story in which the writer's intent is similar to Thurber's, of course you would keep the "moral tag," just as the author wrote it.

The next concern in analysis is to understand the story structure. A simple pattern of story structure is: introduction, initial incident, plot development, climax, and conclusion. Not all stories fit into this pattern, but many do. Figure 2.1 shows a general, uncomplicated pattern that suffices for our discussion of story structure and its importance for the storyteller.

As the diagram suggests, the introduction usually gives the setting, answering the questions, When? Where? Who? and sometimes, What? The initial incident presents the problem, or conflict, and sets the forces into motion. It is the first event in the story which causes the plot to begin to unravel. The plot development, sometimes called "rising action," represents the logical sequence of events that build to the climax, often referred to as the "dramatic climax," or the highest point of interest in the story. The conclusion follows.

Figure 2.1 shows curved lines in the plot development for a specific reason. The incidents leading to the major climax have climaxes themselves, to which you as the storyteller must respond with some intensity. After reaching the peak of an incident you should level off, that is, relax the tension somewhat, before beginning to build with intensity to the next climax. The process of building up and leveling off should continue to the major climax of the story. Interest and suspense should be created progressively as one event leads to another and another, to the highest peak.

If we were to think of the plot development, in the diagram, as a straight line to the top (climax), it would suggest that intensity should increase steadily all the way through the incidents, with no letup, to the climax. This is not desirable, first, because it would tend to create discomfort for the audience rather than pleasurable involvement, and, second, because it

FIG. 2.1. A PATTERN OF A STORY STRUCTURE.

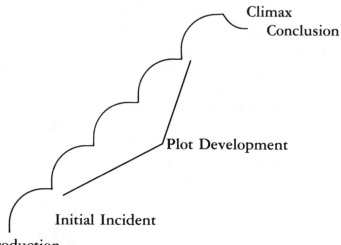

Climax
Conclusion

Plot Development

Initial Incident

Introduction
When? Who?
Where? What?

would tend to cause the storyteller to continuously build with stress and volume, resulting in strain rather than controlled intensity. This is a little like pulling out all of the stops too soon and having no reserves to go further. The curved lines in the plot development of the story structure diagram, then, not only indicate that the story has many minor climaxes leading to the main one, but also suggest the way in which the storyteller should handle climaxes in telling the story.

Figure 2.1 shows the conclusion following quickly after the climax. Many stories, as written, end quickly after the climax with a few statements that neatly tie up the "loose ends." These tales are ideal for the storyteller and pose no problem in telling. Some stories, however, have anticlimactic action — numerous events taking place after the major climax of the story has been reached. It is difficult for a storyteller to hold the interest of an audience when his or her story has anticlimaxes. If your story follows this pattern, or for other reasons seems too long from the climax to the conclusion, note this part of the story for alteration as you proceed with the preparation of the story. (The storyteller's treatment of anticlimaxes and conclusions is discussed next in "Adapting the Story for Telling.")

Understanding the structure of your story is essential since it has direct bearing on the way the story should be told.

ADAPTING THE STORY FOR TELLING

You have studied the story, you know what the author or editor has done with it, and you are now ready to decide what you want to do with it, that is, what will make it most effective for telling. In view of the fact that the story when told will reflect your interpretation of it, it will become partially *your* story. Some stories require no changes for storytelling other than paraphrasing some of the language. However, many require other alterations for various reasons (to be discussed later), and the range of the storyteller's options in adapting a story is wide.

When there is a major alteration in setting, nationality of characters, or other important facets of a story, this change should be made clear to the audience. The storyteller should include the statements in his introduction, acknowledging the liberties he or she has taken with the story. When we present storytellers in a "storytelling hour" for which there is a printed program, we include facts concerning adaptations of stories in print. Examples from the printed storytelling programs are:

"Moki and His Tutu"

The storyteller's free adaptation of
"Epaminondas" to the Hawaiian setting.

"Umetaro"

The storyteller's original story,
based on the Japanese tale,
"Momotaro," or "Peach Boy."

In the "Umetaro" example, only the idea and basic plot of the Japanese folktale "Momotaro" were kept by the teller. "Momotaro" is an excellent story for telling without any major alterations, but in this case, the storyteller wanted to be creative and told a different story, not strictly an adaptation. The story, involving a plum seed instead of a peach, was set in Hawaii and told in local dialect.

Major changes like the one just described for "Momotaro" are the exception rather than the rule. Nevertheless, some changes usually are made, and you should know what the possibilities are. Let's consider the storyteller's editing options: choice of framework; changing from first to third person, or vice-versa, in the telling; changing setting and nationality of characters; deleting plot incidents, minor characters, details, and description; augmenting certain parts; changing narration to dialogue; rearranging plot incidents.

Choice of Framework

A "frame" for storytelling usually consists of an imaginary person, someone other than the storyteller whom the storyteller impersonates suggestively, and an imaginary setting, and imaginary people who would be in such a place. The storyteller quite often will involve his audience, speaking to them and reacting to them as if they were part of the frame of the story. For example, one student took his story from the chapter in Ray Bradbury's *Martian Chronicles* that related the migration of blacks from the southern United States to the planet Mars. He assumed the air of a professor in a lecture hall and started with,

"Now, students, last week we . . . . This week we are concerned with . . . ." At the end of the story he made a comment directly to the audience (again referring to them as students studying a chapter a week), completing the frame. A frame may be established in the beginning without a comment at the end, but this depends on whether the concluding comment will add to or detract from the total effect of the story.

Another storyteller wanted to create the setting of a backwoods country store — the kind of atmosphere Abraham Lincoln may have enjoyed when spinning yarns. So he intimately and directly invited the audience to "Come, draw up that box 'n' rest yerself, I've gotta tale ta tell ya."

Sometimes the author establishes a frame for the story, as in the "Uncle Remus" stories by Joel Chandler Harris. The storyteller may follow through with the frame as presented, if he wishes. Often a frame does not encompass the story, as written, and the storyteller may create a frame for the story if he or she considers it appropriate to do so.

Whether or not to establish a frame for your story is your choice.

Choice of First or Third Person in the Telling

Stories are written in first or third person, probably more often in third person. The speaker, or narrator, may be a major character, minor character, or an observer. More often than not you should follow the cue of the author and tell the story from the point of view he or she has established.

However, you do have the option of changing. When you choose to tell the story in the first person, from the point of view of a major character, then that person becomes dominant and you have to go further with characterization. There is nothing wrong with this, if it is appropriate for the story. Since the story is told from one character's point of view, your role as the storyteller may be limited. While it is good to gain experience in telling stories in the first and third persons, we suggest that you start with the third person, particularly if the story is written this way.

Choice of Changing Setting and Nationality of Characters

We have previously indicated that setting and nationality of characters are changed only on rare occasions. Consider whether you are doing justice to the story by changing the original setting. Some stories fit a particular locale so well that it doesn't seem right to tamper with the setting.

"Pecos Bill," for example, belongs on a Texas ranch, and it would detract from the story to change the setting. But many stories may be adapted to different settings without harm. After all, almost every country has its version of "Cinderella," and we do not know the original settings of many of our best old tales anyway.

Changing the setting, of course, will mean some change in the people, mainly in the way they talk, but the basic characteristics remain. Greed, avarice, kindness, or generosity are the same in New York, London, Hong Kong, and any other place in the world.

Choice of Deleting Plot Incidents, Minor Characters, Details, and Description

In adapting a story, deletion of plot incidents, minor characters, details, and description should be considered. You know that secondary plots and tangents that do not contribute to the central plot should be dropped. These elements are deleted not only because of the time factor involved, but also for the sake of clarity and maintaining interest in telling. Even if a story is not cluttered with secondary plots, some cutting of incidents may be desirable, again for length and interest. For example,

"The Five Chinese Brothers" is a beautiful story, but one student decided to make it shorter by cutting out one of the brothers and the events concerning him. She told the story from his point of view and titled her adaptation, "My Four Chinese Brothers."

As great a story as Rudyard Kipling's "Elephant's Child" is, it does have much anticlimactic action, which makes it difficult for a storyteller to maintain interest from climax to conclusion. Those storytellers who seem to have been most successful with Kipling's story established the advantages of the elephant's long trunk, skipped the experiences that take place during the homeward journey, and finished with the well-rounded conclusion of the story, showing the elephant with his family.

You should not find it necessary to drop incidents and characters from a story as often as you will need to cut some of the description and detail. With experience you will learn that some audiences warm to description more than others, and you will be able to respond to their reactions by cutting or enlarging to some extent on the spot. When you have not memorized your script word for word (and we urge you not to), you will more easily be able to do this spontaneous editing.

We are more concerned here, however, with the details and description as written. Decide what details and description are really necessary or most helpful in the story as told. You can make changes as you go through the other steps in preparing the story. Many of the "he saids" should be dropped once it is clear who is speaking. Generally, in dialogue, if you reply angrily with a character's lines, you will not need to add, "she replied angrily." Do not interpret this suggestion to delete "he saids" and similar remarks as an absolute, because there are times when such statements should be included not only for clarity but for rhythm of speech or for emphasis of the idea.

Choice of Augmenting Certain Parts

The storyteller more often than not should delete description and detail rather than adding to it. But if he wants to make some parts stand out more, especially the climax, he can enlarge with detail, description, and dialogue. Some folktales, or versions of them, have been printed with only the bare essentials. If such is the case with the tale you choose, you should augment, fill in, or build up the details, keeping in mind, of course, appropriateness to character and plot.

Choice of Changing Narration to Dialogue

In general, audiences become more interested in a story when dialogue is mixed with narration. Characters become more real when the characters speak to each other. Most stories have dialogue but many have very little, and once in a while you may find a story with no dialogue. It is a simple matter to turn some of the narration into dialogue. The following is a sample of such a change, using a part of the Greek myth about Persephone for demonstration.

Narration	Narration with Dialogue
After Persephone's disappearance, her mother, Demeter, wandered over the earth searching for news of Persephone. On the tenth night she saw Hecate, who told Demeter that she had heard Persephone's scream and the sound of chariot wheels, but that she had seen nothing.	After Persephone's disappearance, her mother, Demeter, wandered over the earth searching for news of Persephone. On the tenth night she saw Hecate. Demeter called to her, "Hecate, Hecate, can you help me? Have you seen my daughter?"
Hecate went with Demeter to find Apollo, who traversed	"I have not seen Persephone, but I heard her scream, and I heard the sound of chariot

the entire earth each day and saw everything.

Apollo told Demeter what had happened, that Hades had taken Persephone down to his underworld kingdom.

Upon hearing this Demeter wept bitterly, for she knew her daughter was indeed lost to her.

wheels. I heard but could not see from my cave."

"Thank you, Hecate."

Hecate went with Demeter to find Apollo, who traversed the entire earth each day and saw everything. Demeter stopped him, "Apollo, in your travels have you heard or seen anything of Persephone?"

"Yes, yes, I have news, but it is not good. Hades took your daughter down to his underworld kingdom."

"Oh, no, no! Hades! Then she is lost, lost to me!" And Demeter wept bitterly.

Choice of Rearranging Plot Incidents

Most stories are written in a logical sequence of events or in the order an author intended. When secondary plots have been deleted for telling or some other cutting has been done, the storyteller might find rearranging advantageous to his or her plan. Deciding to place the story in a frame employing the "flashback" technique could be another reason for some rearrangement.

"Flashback" means establishing a scene in the present, while episodes of an earlier time are recalled. For example, an old man might say to his grandchild, "I remember a long time ago, before you or your father was born. . . ." Time flashes back to the time in which the story begins. The storyteller's occasions for rearranging plot incidents are rare, perhaps the most infrequently applied option, but you should know that it is a possibility.

After you have analyzed your story and decided what you want to do with it, it is time to set your plan down on paper, a plan that is an outline of the essentials, not all the detail and description. The outline, which we call the "analysis paper," should include:

> Title
> Author (if known)
> Source
> One-sentence character description of major
>   characters
> Statement of theme (sentence form)
> Outline of story
>   introduction
>   initial incident
>   plot development
>   other incidents
>
>   _____
>   _____
>   _____
>
>   climax
>   conclusion

A sample analysis paper follows:

Story Analysis

Title:	"The Peddler and His Caps" (old folktale)
Author:	Unknown
Source:	*Storytelling* by Ruth Tooze
Characters:	Peddler, a run-of-the-mill little man, neither old nor young, experienced in selling, not especially ambitious but concerned over his own property and rights.

	Monkeys, fun-loving, clever, imitative, full of "monkey shine."
Theme:	Monkeys will be monkeys! Or, monkeys see, monkeys do!
Introduction:	Once upon a time there was a peddler who sold caps. He carried the caps on his head — first his old brown cap, then yellow. . . blue. . . green. . . and RED.
Initial Incident:	One day he couldn't sell a single cap.
Plot Development:	He walked to the edge of the village and settled himself under a tree for a nap. Before sleep he checked his caps. . . yellow. . .

He went to sleep and slept for a long time. When he awoke his first thought was of his caps. . .

They were gone!

He looked in front. . . left. . . right. . . around the tree. . . no caps.

Finally looked up in tree, saw monkeys, and every monkey had on one of his caps.

"You monkeys you," shaking his finger.

"Give me back my caps." But the monkeys only shook their fingers. "Tsk, tsk, tsk!"

"You monkeys." This time he shook his fist. "Tsk, tsk, tsk!" (mocking)

"You monkeys." He stamped his foot. "Tsk. . ."

"You monkeys." He stamped both feet.

By now he was very angry — "You monkeys" — and he tore his old brown cap from his head and threw it on the ground.

Climax: And every monkey tore the cap from its head
                and threw it to the ground.

Conclusion: The peddler picked up his caps. . . brown. . .
                yellow. . . blue. . . green. . . and on the tip
                top. . . red. Back to village.
                "Caps for sale!" "Caps. . ."

CHAPTER THREE

Working for Fluency

By NOW YOU HAVE adapted the story and outlined the plan you expect to follow. A copy of the outline should be used as a guide while you are working for fluency. Do not feel bound by what you have on paper. During this and the following steps, changes still may be made, although they should be minor rather than major ones.

OBJECTIVES

Strive for fluency with two objectives in mind: first, to memorize the story sequence — the things that happen in proper order; second, to develop a flow of language without memorizing word for word. Of course, some words, phrases, and refrains (your own and the author's) you will memorize, but it is important that you approach this step by warning yourself, "Don't memorize every word." Remember, you want the final product to sound fresh and spontaneous. Fluency means having sufficient command of the spoken language without having to grope for an idea or a word. This does not mean that your speech should flow so rapidly that no regard is given to pauses and variations in tempo. In fact, the storyteller is sometimes more effective when he or she does seem to think and search a moment for just the right word to express the thought or to paint the picture.

REHEARSALS

In the "fluency" step of preparation, set up three rehearsal sessions in a place in which you feel free to rehearse aloud without restraint. The same length of time spaced over three intervals is more valuable than equal time in one session. At this point, an audience, even one person, is not desirable. However, in these practice sessions and all subsequent ones without an audience, do imagine an audience with whom you intimately communicate.

For the first session, divide the story roughly into three parts. You will be concerned with the first third of the story in this session. From the outline take note of what happens in getting the story started and the events that logically follow. With these in mind you may want to reread the written version of this part of the story. After checking your outline and script, turn them over or lay them aside where you cannot read from them. Now, imagine an audience and tell — talk through — the first third of the story, never looking at the outline or script even if you forget some things. Muddle on through to the end of that third and then consult the outline and the script if you wish. Remember, you are telling the story with details that enlarge on the written outline.

For a second time, set aside the written outline and script, visualize the audience, and tell the first third of the story again. You are not likely to forget the same things in this telling that you left out in the first, and you may be surprised at how much

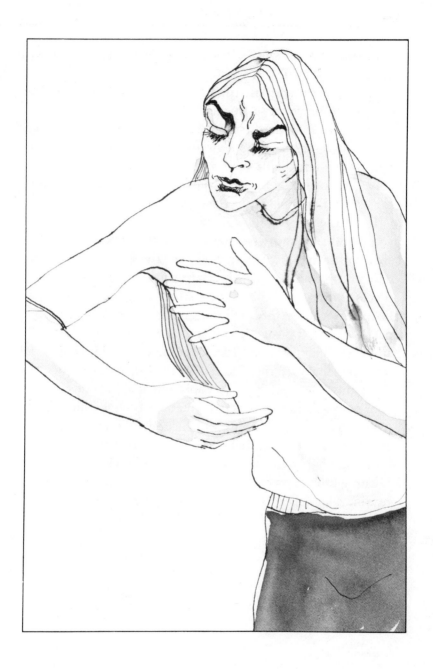

more smoothly the story flows. Again check whatever you wish in event and detail.

For the third and last time, in this first rehearsal, tell the story to an imaginary audience.

You have told the first third of the story three times and should have mastered the logical sequence of happenings, certain important details, and a flow and control of language. Now you should be free to make changes as necessary "on the spot" in telling this part of the story later.

Leave the story now. (Of course, you don't really leave it; you carry it around with you in your subconscious as you go about other matters.) At another time the same day or the next day, set up your second rehearsal session and repeat the above process with the second part of the story. When you have finished with the third telling of that portion of the story, put parts one and two together, telling them once to an imaginary audience. The third and last rehearsal session for fluency follows the same pattern, followed by a telling of the entire story.

At this point you will probably feel good about the shape your story is taking. Although you have been working for two major objectives — learning sequence and developing language smoothness — other things have been happening such as the building of climaxes and development of characters. Let this learning process take place naturally. It will contribute to your readiness for concentrated effort on further steps of preparation described next.

CHAPTER FOUR

Working for Characterization

INITIALLY STUDENTS SEEM MORE fearful or insecure in dealing with characterization than any other aspect of storytelling. After experience with it, however, many find characterization the most satisfying element of the storyteller's craft.

"Must I be an actor to be a good storyteller?" students often ask. The answer is no, but the storyteller does need to use imagination and drop inhibitions insofar as it is possible. He or she has to identify and distinguish the various characters sufficiently for the audience to create the characters in their own minds. To achieve this, some traits of the characters need to be made apparent to the audience through the visible and audible behavior of the storyteller. In the final product, characterization is one part (albeit an important part) of a unified whole.

UNDERSTANDING STORY CHARACTERS

Your analysis of the story included some character analysis, but at this stage in preparation you should focus full attention

on the characters of the story in order to gain a deeper understanding of each one. As you do so, try to imagine how you can
convey each to an audience.

1. *Character traits.* For each character in the story, ask questions like the following: What kind of person or character is he
or she? Honest? Kind? Deceitful? Sly? Intelligent? Formally
educated? Experience educated? Insecure? Confident? What do
the characters say and do that give clues to the kinds of persons
they are? What does the author say about the characters that
may give clues to their personalities?

2. *Motivations of the characters.* What motivates each of the
characters? What makes them tick? Consider the broad general
motivations, like a person's tendency to stinginess, and then
the specific ones, such as a person's reaction to seeing a coin
drop from a stranger's pocket.

3. *Relation to other characters.* What is the relation of each
character to every other one? Who are his or her friends?
Enemies? What are the family relationships?

4. *Purpose of the character in the story.* Finally, what purpose
does each character serve in the story? Is he or she a main
character around whom the action centers? Is that person a
minor character whose purpose is more of an observer?

Answering questions such as these should lead to deeper
understanding of the people in the story and should also help
to keep the characters in appropriate balance in your telling.

Visualizing Characters

Form a mental picture of what each character looks like and
imagine how each sounds. Then consider what traits may be emphasized in order to bring out contrasts among the characters.

1. *Physical appearance.* If the author has not given a complete physical description of each character, or if the clues are

not sufficient to give you a total picture, decide for yourself each character's height, weight, sex, coloring, age, etc.

2. *Voice and speech style.* Imagine that you hear the character speak. Is the voice gruff, low in pitch, forceful, or what? Does his speech reflect education, sophistication? What about the tempo of speech? Is it fast? Slow?

3. *Contrasts in characterization.* After you have created a mental picture of all the characters, think about the major differences among them. For example, one character may have a rather slow tempo in speech and movement, whereas another has a fast pace in speech and jerkiness in movement. Note these differences now. Later, when you prepare for the actual development of the story's characters, you will use this knowledge.

4. *Animals and natural elements.* Fables, and some folktales and fairy tales have animals endowed with human characteristics such as speech. Indeed, human characteristics may be given to all of nature — wind, fire, water, sun, trees, and stones. Animals and the natural elements are both a great challenge and great fun for the storyteller. Imagine the sly fox, the slithery snake, the furry rabbit, the prickly porcupine, and the hard, crusty turtle acting like humans!

A student in a workshop once asked, "I've got a turtle in my story, an important character, but what can I do with a turtle?" From the members of the workshop came such ideas as: "I think of a turtle as being hard all over." "Yeah, very slow moving." "Except the head that kind of darts out of the hard crust." "Could you keep your body stiff as though it were confined in an unrelenting hollow, steel shell?" "Right, sense the steel shell especially from the back of the neck, over the shoulders and down." "Then you wouldn't move the body at all except for your head, 'turtle head' fashion." "Yes, unless you have reason for the whole turtle to move, in which case it would be a one-piece slow movement."

Soon the storyteller began to contribute many of the ideas, suggestions for visible and audible behavior which spurred her on to experiment with body and voice. Her final characterization of the turtle turned out to be effective and appropriate when she told the story.

How to Work for Characterization

Although the results of characterization are different in telling a story aloud to an audience and acting out characters in play form, the procedure for working on characterization may be much the same. The widely ranging suggestions for developing characters generally fall into two schools of thought: the "outside-in" approach, stemming from the "mechanical" school, and the "inside-out" approach, credited to Stanislavsky and his colleagues of the "natural" school.

The outside-in approach suggests that once the performer has decided what a character looks like — for example, a hunched-over, unsteady, old man — he or she deliberately places his or her body in a corresponding posture by bending the back, rounding the shoulders, bending the knees slightly, keeping the elbows close to the body, and causing the hands to quiver. Once in this position, the performer will begin to feel like an old man inside, thinking his thoughts and evoking his emotions.

The inside-out theory promotes the opposite approach of the mechanical one. Believers in this approach suggest that the performer think the thoughts of the character, take his or her emotional attitude, and talk from the character's point of view. When the performer does so, his or her body will automatically, or naturally, manifest the posture and actions of the character being portrayed.

Critics of the outside-in approach point to the extreme use of this method as being artificial, not only being mechanical in approach but remaining so in performance. Critics of the inside-out approach point to the extreme use of this method as being void of any technique, consequently leaving the performer to the mercy of chance in portraying the desired emotions and traits of character.

Undoubtedly either approach when utilized as intended has been a successful method of developing character for many actors. We prefer a combination of the two methods, that is, the simultaneous use of both. Storytellers should try all of these approaches and then use whatever seems to work best for them.

DEVELOPING CHARACTERS

With this background on approaches to characterization in mind, let's proceed to the process of developing characters for storytelling.

Experimenting with Body and Voice

Feel free to use as much space as you like — a whole room for moving around. Take one character at a time from your story and concentrate on developing the role as if you were playing no other. Walk all over the room to get a sense of the rhythm in the movement of the character to help you establish his characteristics, even though in the actual telling of your story for an audience you might take no more than one or two steps as this character. For example, imagine the giant in "Jack and the Beanstalk." He's freakishly big, heavy, cumbersome, awkward, and probably moves more slowly than a smaller person. As you think these things about the giant, start to move as a giant would — heavily, noisily, planting the feet firmly as you stride about. Let your arms come out a bit from the torso to help give the illusion of bigness. While you continue to move, begin to speak as the giant, either saying something he actually says in the story or something you improvise.

Because you are thinking and moving as the giant, your voice may almost automatically be correspondingly big, forceful, and low in pitch. If it isn't, then experiment with your voice, purposely lowering the pitch and holding the vowel sounds longer. Assume the attitude of anger for the giant, moving in his rhythm, and voicing his refrain, "Fee, fie, fo, fum, I smell the blood of an Englishman."

You don't have to have a bass voice to convincingly suggest the giant. A woman can use the lower tones of her voice range and increase the volume. If attitude, body reaction, and timing are appropriate for the giant, the overall desired effect will be achieved. By the way, don't force or strain your voice in working for characterization. First, this could be detrimental to your voice; and, second, if it sounds strained, even though it does not hurt, it will cause the audience to be uncomfortable and thus defeat your purpose.

Men should not use an unnaturally high pitched voice to suggest women and children. Such a practice burlesques characterization. Only if your intention is to project broad humor or slapstick should you use an unusually high pitched voice. And in general, a male storyteller is more effective with most audiences if he does not attempt to impersonate women, either with a forced, high voice or with exaggerated feminine mannerisms. Instead he should focus attention on the attitude and outstanding personality traits of the woman. Then he is likely to use a thinner voice, still within his own natural range. Add the woman character's language and rhythm, particularly voice inflections, and a man should have a strong enough suggestion of character through voice to convince his audience.

If you are a male storyteller dealing with female body actions, think and work with characteristics that are appropriate for the specific character regardless of her gender, rather than contrived characteristics that seem to play up general

female body posturing — that is, unless the purpose is to draw
a caricature rather than suggest a believable character.

As you experiment with each character (after the fashion of
the "giant" example), emphasize the traits in one character that
are different from those of another. You noted the differences
earlier; now is the time to make the differences apparent in
your characterization.

Scenes with Dialogue

When you experimented with body and voice for characterization, you may or may not have used actual conversation from
your story. At this point, however, you should be concerned
with the specific conversations that you have planned to include in the telling of your story. Therefore, pick out all of the
scenes in which there is conversation. These scenes will be used
as you continue the process of working for characterization.

One Character at a Time

Begin with a scene that has no more than two characters
talking to each other, and concentrate on one of the characters
all the way through the conversation. In other words, when one
character (let's call him A) speaks, imagine that the other
character, B, is there in front of him. Establish the placement
of character B slightly off center and over the heads of the
imaginary audience. Place him by focusing left or right, but for
the duration of this scene, when you look at B, be consistent
with placement. That is, every time it is appropriate to look
into the eyes of B, see him in the spot you have established
for him.

For characterization in a specific scene, you are concentrating on A in this practice session. Assume the physical and
vocal traits of A which you have already developed, and practice his or her lines for a particular conversation. Feel free to
repeat lines and change the way you say them until you are

satisfied with the results. Between speeches, stay in character and briefly listen and react to character B's lines. B's lines (which you hear only in your imagination) are motivation for A's speeches.

After spending some time with character A, you will feel that he is beginning to live. Now it is time to work with character B. Note that if you placed B slightly to the right when you were working on A's lines, you should place A slightly to the left as you work on B's lines.

Continue working with characters separately in all conversations in the story. When you have a third character in a conversation, practice his lines separately, as you have the others. For placement, have the third character, C, look slightly left to speak to A only, right to speak to B. If his speech is for both A and B, look directly center. When A speaks to B and C together, look slightly right, as you did to speak to B alone. The opposite holds for B speaking to A and C.

Character placement should not be a problem when working with one character at a time. It is important, however, that you place the characters "out front," that is, toward the audience.

Characters Interacting

Placement of characters becomes more complicated when they interact. Working on the characters separately should serve to help you put them together in a conversation. Your task is to make the talking appear as natural and believable as possible and to move the story along with the conversation. The listener, one hopes, will become more involved in the story because of the characterization and dialogue. The task tends to become most difficult for the storyteller when the dialogue is made up of one-word or one-line speeches between the characters. Obviously the one-liners call for quick subtle changes in point of view. The demand for quick character changes points up the fact that you cannot portray the story characters as you would play a single character on stage.

As the storyteller, you play all roles — the narrator and all of the characters. It follows, then, that you should suggest the characters, through voice and body, sufficiently enough for the audience to complete the pictures of the characters and their actions in their own imaginations. For example, if the action in a play script indicates "John goes to the window," the actor would walk to the window. But if this were an important action in a story, the storyteller would say, "John goes to the window." While saying the line he would tense his muscles as if he were going to take the first step forward. Presto! We are at the window, ready to visualize whatever is happening there.

In developing a particular character, you were advised to work as if you were playing no other. But now, since you must deal with several characters and narration, broad actions will call for more subtle treatment. Suppose your story includes an old man. When you worked on developing this character, you decidedly hunched the shoulders over. Now that he is inter-acting with another character in short exchanges, perhaps even "cutting in" on some lines, you do not have the time to hunch over as much. However, some trace of that posture is likely to be there as you speak with his attitude and his voice.

Angles and Levels in Character Placement

When you worked with individual characters in a scene, you imagined and placed the character addressed by looking at him slightly to the right or left of center over the heads of your audience. Let's say that as the king you look slightly to the right to see Jason and as Jason you look slightly to the left to see the king. You should *not* call attention to this technique by turning from side to side.

Some beginners, in working with character placement, feel the desire to actually move several steps to the right when giving one character's lines and then several steps to the left when changing to another character. The desire is understandable and suggests that the beginner is aware of the need to distinguish his characters. But the practice of moving from side to side to denote change of characters calls undesirable attention to a mechanical device. It is likely to produce a comic effect.

The storyteller should keep the angles narrow in shifting from one character to another. Often a shift of the eyes with no shift of the head, much less the body, is all the indication of a change in placement that is needed. We are referring only to the technical angle in placement here, not to the always desirable change in voice and body to suggest different characters. The stronger the suggestion of character through voice and body, the more narrow may be the angle and the less need for any angle.

While training, the storyteller should try to master the technique of character placement and angles whether he always employs them in future storytelling or not. Consider figure 4.1. The lines on either side of the center show how slight the change in eye direction from side to side should be in conversation.

When we talk with someone, we seldom keep our eyes glued to his for a long period. More often we begin speaking by looking into the eyes, glancing away sometimes to reflect over what we have heard, and coming back to the eyes. Be guided by the same behavior in the story, depending on the people and the situation. After placing a character in a certain spot at eye level, be consistent throughout a given scene or conversation by coming back to that spot whenever you want to establish eye-to-eye contact with him or her.

Fig. 4.1. Character Placement.

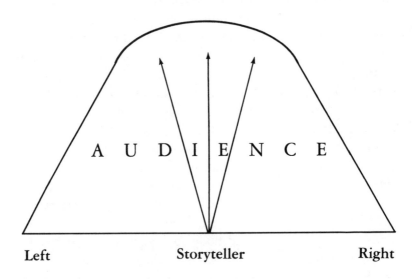

Left   Storyteller   Right

Suggestions for placement of three characters in a conversation were previously given, but now that you are working on interaction of characters the information bears repeating. Consider figure 4.1 again. Let's say we have characters A, B, and C. A looks off-center right to see B. B looks off-center left to see A. C looks center front to see A and B together. If he directs his speech particularly to A he glances slightly left, right for B. A looks right to speak to C and B together. He makes a slight adjustment, still to right, to speak to either one singly. B looks left to speak to C and A together or singly.

The storyteller should also be aware of vertical placement. For adults, unless there is an unusual difference in height, there should be little or no difference in eye level as you look from one to the other. In talking to a small child, an adult would lower the eye level a little. Look at what would be the level of a child's eyes. The closer he or she is to you, the lower your eye level drops. A child looking at a giant's face would look way up, but not to the ceiling.

Naturally, if your characters are in a situation calling for high and low positions, you must adjust your eye level accordingly. For instance, in "The Peddler and His Caps," the peddler looks up to talk to the monkeys in the tree, and they look down to respond to him. A person lying on a bed or sitting looks up to see and talk with a person who is standing. As a storyteller, you should indicate these physical relationships through appropriate eye level.

Maximum of Three Characters in Conversation

It is difficult for a storyteller to effectively portray and distinguish more than three characters talking together. We are referring to a limit on the number of characters in conversation with one another, not to a limit of the number of characters who might be in a scene.

About this point, one student asked, "In my story, a mother goat lines up her seven little kids and talks to them. It's important that there be seven kids. What should I do?" The reply was that there need be little difference in characterization of the kids. A couple of spokesmen for the seven kids could easily carry all of their lines. It was also suggested that the storyteller, in the character of the mother goat, might line the kids up in front of her (the imagined line would be between storyteller and audience). The mother could make it clear that she was talking to all seven kids, perhaps numbering each one as she looks at it.

On those rare occasions when you find it important that more than three characters talk to one another, you may need to turn some of the dialogue into narration or intersperse the dialogue with narration. These points are discussed in "Devices That Aid Characterization."

Freedom to Feel, Talk, and React

Because much has been said about the limitations in angles during the interaction of characters, you may think that all characterization in storytelling is to be restricted. This is not the case. In dealing with any given character, as character and storyteller, you should feel free to walk, talk, and react in any way that seems appropriate to the character and his or her particular role in the story and appropriate for you as the storyteller. We avoid rules that tend to draw sharp boundary lines. This book places storytelling on a continuum of speech communication, which suggests much overlapping of the arts. The range of behavior for character portrayal in storytelling is wide and may overlap with impersonation. Behavior of the storyteller in characterization varies depending on the story itself, the audience, and the storyteller.

The types of characters and their importance in any given story will affect the degree of characterization to be used. By the same token, your audience will affect the character's behavior. In general, young children like big movements and broad portrayal of characters. A short story for adults generally calls for less broad characterization and more subtle inferences.

The degree of characterization differs according to the individual storyteller. One person may portray the characters in a story with much overt action, with broad treatment for each character, yet with smooth interchanging of characters and appropriate blending of characters into the story. Another person telling the same story may portray the characters in a much more subtle fashion, with little overt action, yet with fine distinctions between them and a keen awareness of everything happening in the story. The two storytellers, though quite different in their portrayal of characters, may be equally effective with the total story.

The Storyteller and Dramatic Scenes

The storyteller should not allow long, dramatic scenes to separate him or her from the audience. Scenes that have considerable dialogue and little or no narration tend to become detached, and the storyteller must find ways to minimize this separateness. If your story has such scenes, try inserting a few words as the storyteller, words that help to move the scene along and at the same time serve to acknowledge the audience. Your attitude is also important. Your primary goal is to create an imaginative world for your listeners and a feeling in them of belonging in that world. Sometimes just a glance at the audience, a nod of your head, or the expression of your eyes and face say, "We are there." The scene and the characters then, will be more a part of the story.

Merging Narration and Character

When a character is being introduced by the narrator or when the narration describes the way the character feels or what he or she is doing prior to dialogue, the storyteller should begin to sound and react from the character's point of view in the narration. This is to prepare the audience for the character and involve them in the story. For example, let's take the giant in "Jack and the Beanstalk." The narration leading into his dialogue might go something like this: "The giant arrived home. He was in a foul mood. He kicked open the door, sniffed the air, and yelled, 'Fee, fie, fo, fum, I smell the blood of an Englishman!'"

The storyteller should express a foul mood and begin to sound like the giant by the time he says "foul mood," and then proceed to seem more like the giant as he leads into the giant's lines. In this way, an abrupt booming of the giant is avoided and a smooth blending of narration and character is accomplished.

Devices That Aid Characterization

Several devices, mainly involving minor editing, may be helpful in working with characterization. The following examples are presented in writing, but once you understand the principles involved, you will be able to apply some of them verbally, without using a script.

Narration mixed with dialogue helps the storyteller in making distinctions in character. Most writers of stories do mix the narration and dialogue, making it easier for the storyteller to distinguish characters and keeping the presentation within the storyteller's realm. Notice the mixture of dialogue and narration in the following excerpt from "The Golden Fleece":

The people had now withdrawn from around him so that the young man stood in an open space, near the smoking altar, front to front with the angry King Pelias.

"Who are you?" ~~cried the king, with a terrible frown.~~ "And how dare you make this disturbance while I am sacrificing a black bull to my father, Neptune?"

"It is no fault of mine," ~~answered Jason.~~ "Your Majesty, you must blame the rudeness of your subjects, they who have raised all the tumult because one of my feet happens to be bare."

When Jason said this, the king gave a quick, startled glance down at his feet.

"Ha!" muttered he, "Here is the one-sandaled fellow, sure enough! What can I do with him?"

As we pointed out previously, many "he said" derivatives should be deleted from the narration. Note the cuts in the sample above: "cried the king, with a terrible frown" and "answered Jason."

Calling the name of the person addressed, especially in the initial speech of a conversation, also aids character distinction. The name or title may be inserted by the storyteller in character, or a slight rearrangement of words will often achieve the same effect. Take an example from the excerpt above:

Original	Rearrangement
"It is no fault of mine," answered Jason. "Your Majesty must blame the rudeness of your subjects."	"Your Majesty, it is no fault of mine. You must blame the rudeness of your subjects."

This is the first of Jason's speeches to the king. By simply moving "Your Majesty" to the beginning, the storyteller makes clear to the audience who is speaking to whom.

Directives that cut into short speeches may be better arranged as part of the narrative to introduce the speech. Thus:

When Jason said this, the king gave a quick, startled glance down at his feet.
(add) He muttered, "Ha!"
(cut) muttered he

The last of the narration which precedes dialogue should call attention to the character who speaks first. To do so, you may frequently need to rearrange the wording or add a word or two in order to bring attention to the appropriate character. Note in the example above how the narrative leads into the dialogue. The focus is on the king, his reaction, what he does, and the way he speaks before he says anything. We are not misled by having Jason speak.

The devices discussed above (mixing narration with dialogue, cutting or adding directives, rearranging directives, and naming the person addressed) should be thought of as supporting and refining elements. They cannot replace the appropriate attitude and imaginative characterization of the storyteller, but they may aid in clarity and overall effectiveness of characterization.

CHAPTER FIVE

Working for Visualization

WEBSTER'S SEVENTH NEW COLLEGIATE Dictionary defines *visualize* as: "to make or become visible; or to see or form a mental image of." *Imagine* is comparably defined: "to form a mental image." *Image* means "a mental representation of anything not actually present to the senses." Visualization as a step in the preparation of a story involves the storyteller's response to images inherent in the language of the story, a vivid re-creation of mental images, and skill in projecting the images to an audience. Through audible and visible behavior, the storyteller seeks to convey the setting, characters, action, feeling, tone, and mood of the story so as to create in the listener's mind a mental image of what is taking place each moment of the story. A moving picture of each scene should flash through the listener's mind as the teller relates the tale.

IMPORTANCE OF VISUALIZATION FOR
THE STORYTELLER

Without the development and use of visualization, the storyteller becomes nothing more than a relater of incidents. After a short time, no matter how arresting the series of incidents, most listeners become bored. With visualization heightened, incidents come alive. A quality of "nowness" is established which brings the audience into the never-never land that the storyteller is creating.

By a quality of "nowness," we mean the assimilating or reliving of the story by the interpreter to the extent that the things being talked about, though they may have occurred hundreds of years ago, seem to come alive now for the audience as it hears the story. When the storyteller projects vivid mental pictures of Robin Hood, for instance, who lived his imaginary life in England's Sherwood Forest, the character of Robin Hood should live again for the audience. The listeners should have the feeling that they are there — now. In their mind's eye they will see the world of Robin Hood, the woods and the rest of his environment, the characters surrounding him, and the action taking place. They should empathize and become physically and mentally involved, just as the storyteller is involved.

Most people probably know someone who has been able to immediately carry his listeners into the imaginary world of the story he is telling. Such people are not always physically impressive or appealing. The late Charles Laughton, a famous actor and storyteller, was a pudgy man, with irregular, nondescript features, but from the moment he approached his audience he commanded attention through purposeful attitude. He was so keenly sensitive to imagery that his visible and audible behavior drew attention to the material, not to himself. On one storytelling occasion, he leaned toward the audience and said with all of the exhilaration of the moment, "Wasn't that good?" He was experiencing and enjoying the story completely and hoped his audience shared that "good" feeling.

IMAGERY

In order to evoke the desired response from your listeners, you must stimulate them through one or more of their senses. The only senses through which you can reach your listeners directly are the visual and auditory ones. Your audience can see you (your posture, movements, facial expressions, and other gestures), and they can hear what you say and how you say it. Nevertheless, you can indirectly stimulate all types of sensation by imagery, through the use of words that have the power of producing imagined sensations in the one who hears them. Written words create images for the reader. He can imagine the bitterness of quinine, the caress of a lover's hand, the rhythm of the dance, the dizziness of height, the faint tolling of the bells, a deeply grooved and weather-beaten face, for example. But when these written symbols are spoken aloud, the possibilities of creating sensory images are much greater.

To achieve the visualization of images in the listener's mind, you should strive for clear pictures in your own mind. Identifying imagery is one way of increasing your awareness of and sensitivity to the images in written symbols.

Imagery has been classified in different ways. Most classifications include a listing of those images perceived through the senses of sight, hearing, smell, taste, and touch. Other lists add temperature, thirst, pain, movement, balance, and hunger as sensory images. Nonsensory images are sometimes listed as kinesthetic, emotional, and imaginative.

There is no fixed list of images, and you may want to work out your own chart for labeling purposes. In the examples that appear in the next section, the following types of imagery are used.

1. *Visual* (things seen): e.g., the glowing lights of an onrushing automobile.

2. *Auditory* (things heard): e.g., the shriek of a woman.

3. *Gustatory* (things tasted): e.g., the sourness of a pickle.

4. *Olfactory* (things smelled): e.g., the delightful aroma of a fresh rose.

5. *Tactile* (things touched): e.g., the soft, plush feel of velvet.

6. *Kinesthetic* (muscular reaction): e.g., a woman's pressed lips; (larger movement): e.g., a running boy.

7. *Thermal* (temperature): e.g., a piping hot potato.

8. *Equilibrium* (balance): e.g., a tightrope walker.

9. *Organic* (internal sensations): e.g., the faintness of hunger, the sharpness of pain; (emotional responses): e.g., the fear of the unknown, the surprise of discovery.

Suggestions for Developing Visualization

Many storytellers react to imagery without being conscious that they are doing so. In their preparation for storytelling, they may not have been aware that they were responding to olfactory, tactile, or other forms of imagery. Yet in telling their stories, these people do establish a quality of nowness.

However, other storytellers find visualization illusive, even when consciously working with it. One such student was struggling with this aspect of storytelling in a workshop. She was doing a poor job of describing a long, carpeted room leading to a king's throne and was told, "Susan, look at the floor. Do you see that red carpet stretching all the way back to the wall?" She looked at the floor for a moment, then at the interrogator, and answered matter-of-factly, "No, I'm sorry, but I only see a brown vinyl tile floor." She obviously failed to imagine in her own mind what she wanted the others to see and consequently failed also to project the sensation to others.

Heightened Perception

Almost everyone has imagination. Many, however, suppress it and inhibit the responses to what is sensed. To convey images as storytellers, therefore, we first need to break down the barriers, and then consciously try to respond to the stimuli around us.

To become more aware, pay attention to what you see, hear, touch, taste, smell. Decide that for thirty minutes to an hour each day you will notice in detail the things and people around you. Afterward, try to recall what you sensed over that period of time by describing these sensations to yourself or to someone else. Next, concentrate on one sense, such as touch. Carefully feel an object of some sort with your eyes closed. To another person witnessing your experience, tell as much as you can about the object from the feeling you get of it. Try similar activities with the other senses. Such activities are ways of increasing awareness and, one hopes, of stimulating imagination.

This observation-recall process needs to be carried further if it is to aid the storyteller significantly. For example, it is not enough just to remember that you once smelled fried chicken. When you say "fried chicken," can you smell it? Could you orally re-create that sensation for a listener? To do so is important to the storyteller. If he says "dizzy" and can feel it, says "lemon" and can taste it and says "green rolling hills" and sees them, his voice and body will react naturally to the sensations and pictures, and usually cause the audience to respond similarly.

Identifying Images

Finding and labeling images should help you to be more aware of them. In order to learn how to label images, try this method: Choose a short segment of a story. The initial incident is a good place to begin. Then label the kinds of imagery you find. For example, in the following excerpt from John Steinbeck's *The Winter of Our Discontent,* the images are labeled as suggested.

> The ground swell on the rising tide whished into the place [visual and tactile] and raised my legs and hips and swung them to the side [kinesthetic, tactile, organic]. I rolled on one hip and reached in my side pocket for my razor blades and I felt the lump [kinesthetic, tactile, organic]. Then in wonder I remembered the caressing, stroking hands of the light bearer [organic, tactile].[1]

Stressing Key Images

Most stories contain a great deal of imagery. For example, the short segment from Steinbeck quoted above is full of imagery — several kinds in each sentence. In a typical story, although replete with imagery, certain images are meant to be more important than others. Read the Steinbeck segment again. Note the phrase "I felt the lump." If you had read the entire novel, you would know the importance of the "lump" at this point of the story. The "lump," a talisman, is extremely important to this character. It saves him from taking his life. The images conveyed by the words, "I felt the lump," are the vital ones in that passage. They need to stand out in the listener's mind above all of the other images that appear. The storyteller's job is to make the vital images vivid to the listener. Otherwise, part of the intended meaning may be lost. So, a careful analysis of a story's imagery is essential in picking out the key images.

---

[1]From *The Winter of Our Discontent* by John Steinbeck. Copyright © 1961 by John Steinbeck. Reprinted by permission of Viking Penguin, Inc.

While the important images are stressed, the remaining ones need attention so that the scene described by the author flashes through the listener's head. In the Steinbeck segment, the listener should see and feel the ground swell, the speaker's legs and hips move, and the hand touching the talisman. All of those images should appear, yet the touching of the lump should be sensed by the listener as more important than the others because this is the vital part of the passage.

Projection of Images through Audible and Visible Behavior

No single, proper way exists to practice visualization. The teller will have to devise a method with which he or she feels most comfortable. However, the following procedure may be a useful starting point. Take a portion of a story. Identify the images by labeling them. Determine the most important. Then say the part aloud, letting your imagination run wild as you freely respond through voice and body to the author's words.

As you tell this part, experiment with your voice and body — they should go together and aid each other. For example, practice the line, "Full speed ahead. The tanker's too close. We'll crash. Look out!" Try tensing your muscles as you shout, "Look out!" Repeat and get more force on "out" to convey the warning. In addition to tensing your muscles, lean forward. Try it again, this time raising your hands in warning as you shout, "Look out!" Did it feel appropriate to raise your hands? Or was it better without the added gestures? Use whatever feels best. Next, consider the importance of "look out." Is this phrase the most important one in the passage? Should it be stressed? Or is another phrase more vital? Work through each line in the portion of the story in this manner.

Recognize as you practice that words when said aloud suggest the proper image. "Slow" takes longer to say than "quick" even though "quick" has more sounds in it. When we add to this the connotation usually associated with each of these words, we are likely to take twice as much time in saying "slow" as we do in saying "quick." Even when the word doesn't necessarily sound like its meaning, we can usually bring the desired meaning to it through voice, pitch, inflection, tone, intensity, and duration.

Following is an illustration of how one person prepared and practiced visualization for the Steinbeck segment previously quoted.

> As the storyteller, I remember the dramatic importance of these sentences. The moment has arrived when this person is about to commit suicide. As the narrator, I must establish the point of view of the man. The narration here is in the first person, but even if it were third person, the telling should be from the man's point of view — his thoughts and emotions.
>
> As the storyteller, I am standing; however, the man I am trying to project to the audience is actually lying in the water. What can I do in the standing position to create the image of the man in the appropriate environment?

The ground swell
on the rising tide
whished
into the place
and raised
my legs and hips
and swung them to the
side.

I see the water as I say this and sense the wave rushing to engulf me. My voice and the mental image I get carry this feeling to the audience. I'm not afraid of drowning. The force moves my legs and hips, I don't fight it. I re-create a sense of being moved by water, not by myself, but by painting the image for my audience through my voice — "raised (lift in voice) . . . legs . . . hips . . . swung (prolong; "ng" sings)."

Up to now things have been done to me. Now, I must initiate movement; I'm here to commit suicide. I was thrown to the left side by the water, so I roll more to the left in order to reach my right pocket for the razor blades. I tense the muscles of my entire body and slightly move the right side with more tension, lifting the shoulder to initiate a roll as

I rolled on one hip

I say "rolled." The word rolls out with a circle of "o" and curve of "l." I voice it with a "roll" in anticipation of reach-

and reached

ing for the razor blades.

I've made up my mind to die. I tense my right hand and reach toward my pocket as I

in my side pocket
for my razor blades

say "reached." Would the man reach quickly, slowly, or somewhere in between? I try each and settle on the "in between" pace for the movement. As I reach for the razor blades, I (as the storyteller) know that this man is going to be surprised

and I felt the lump.

to feel the lump, a talisman instead of razor blades. Everything in this scene has led up to this moment. Surprise gives way to a profound inner change of course.

I try saying the line, "and I felt the lump," and then showing surprise and the realization of the significance of the talisman. I try it simultaneously, that is, saying the line, feeling the lump in my hand, and reacting with facial expression. After discovering the razor blades, I react at first without words to feeling the lump in my hand, holding the body very still, with an expression of surprise on my face, and slowly

Then in wonder

say, "and I felt [the facial expression showing the impact of the talisman] the lump."

I pause, holding the image,

I remember
the caressing, stroking
hands of the light bearer.

and then remembering the love of the giver and her caressing hands, I say the last line.

Eye Focus and Visualization

Visualization calls for a different kind of eye focus than that most commonly employed by speakers. Generally, we think of the eye-to-eye contact between speaker and listener as being the most effective eye focus in communicating. The storyteller, however, is concerned with three important types of eye focus: direct eye contact, space visualization, and character-to-character eye contact.

Direct eye contact is the eye-to-eye contact in which the speaker's eyes are focused directly on the eyes of the listeners as he sees them (and he hopes to get a response). As you start to tell a story, just before you speak, your eyes should say, "I have a story I want to share with you." Introductory remarks should be given with direct eye focus. Much of the narration may be appropriately communicated through direct eye contact; however, the amount varies according to the story itself.

Space visualization means looking into space, usually over the heads of an audience, and imagining something — a mental picture of a landscape or action that is taking place in the story being told. Sometimes the listener is better able to create mental images if the storyteller seems to see what he is talking about. For example, he might look at a specific spot in space and see "a green rolling hill" as he says it. But the storyteller should not focus in space for a long time at any one occasion. He must acknowledge his audience every once in a while with a glance or a look that says, "We are enjoying this together, you and I."

Focus in space may also be used to suggest reflection or inner thoughts. In this case, the storyteller does not seem to see anything in a particular place, but his gaze into space suggests that he is thinking. Intersperse the use of space visualization and direct focus. In this way both the highly imaginative elements of the story and intimacy with the audience are maintained.

Character-to-character eye contact means focusing on and seeing the imaginary character addressed. When there is dialogue, the narrator establishes placement for each character, as explained earlier in the section "Working for Characterization." In the conversation, when it is appropriate for one character to see another, the narrator, in character role, looks at a particular spot in space and establishes eye contact with the imaginary character.

CHAPTER SIX

Working for Bodily Action and Control

WHETHER OR NOT THE storyteller knows it, he or she constantly communicates or interacts with the audience on a nonverbal level. Ray Birdwhistell, an expert on nonverbal behavior, estimates that the verbal components of an orally presented message carry less than 35 percent of the meaning; more than 65 percent is carried on the nonverbal level. The word nonverbal is used here to mean all human communication events that transcend the spoken or written word. These events have seven dimensions — body motion, physical characteristics, touch behavior, paralanguage (vocal qualities), proxemics, artifacts, and environment. All of these can be used by the storyteller to support his or her verbal behavior. Unfortunately, the nonverbal may also detract from the speaker's verbal effectiveness.

Four ways nonverbal behavior relates to the teller's story are:

1. *Repeating.* Nonverbal behavior can be used to repeat what is said verbally. For example, if the storyteller says, "Go to the

right!" and points in that direction, he would be repeating nonverbally the verbal message.

2. *Substituting*. Nonverbal behavior can also be used to substitute for verbal messages. For instance, if the teller is relating a story which in its printed form contained the line, "With a shrug of the shoulder, he said . . . ," an actual shrug of the shoulder by the storyteller could substitute for the verbal message and make the utterance of the line unnecessary. The audience should grasp the intended meaning through the nonverbal behavior.

3. *Accenting*. Parts of the story stand out by accenting them nonverbally. For instance, if the story has the line, "No! I don't want to do it!" the storyteller can accent the "No" by stamping his foot, pounding his fist on something, or making some other appropriate physical motion to convey the determination of the speaker in the story.

4. *Contradicting*. The storyteller can contradict his or her spoken message through nonverbal behavior. The classic example is that of the husband with a sneer on his face, a sarcastic vocal quality, and tense posture uttering the words, "I love you," to his wife. Here the nonverbal behavior contradicts the verbal message, and the wife could rightfully interpret the message to mean, "I hate you." The student with a puzzled facial expression responding to the teacher with the words, "Yes, I understand!" is an example common in the classroom. Storytellers must be aware of the "contradiction" phenomenon. They must control their bodily reaction so that it will support, not contradict, the verbal message they relate.

In some stories the author wants the nonverbal behavior to deny the verbal, or vice versa. The author may want the husband, in the classic example just mentioned, to respond nonverbally with hate while mouthing the "I love you" expression. Then the storyteller has to relay the author's intended meaning to the audience by the appropriate nonverbal behavior, conveying this denial of the verbal by accenting, that is, stressing the nonverbal behavior. This should be made so obvious that the audience sees the denial with ease.

To use nonverbal behavior as a means of strengthening the telling of the story, the storyteller should plan and practice. However, when the story is told to an audience, the nonverbal behavior should not look planned. Rather, it should appear spontaneous. Body language must be purposeful and supportive.

Recall the previous section on visualization. A suggestion was made there on how to discover imagery in your story: go through your selection and mark off the types of imagery contained in it. As you do this, determine the sorts of nonverbal behavior you could use to strengthen your story, to enhance the imagery, and to convey the meaning and feeling.

Recognize that the storyteller does not go so far as to act out what is happening. The nonverbal behavior used should not reach the extreme of mimicking what is occurring in the story, thus calling the audience's attention to the physical action. Rather, it should help create images inherent in the story. For example, if your story refers to parts of the body such as the eyes, ears, and nose, you should not point to them as they are mentioned unless they are vital to the plot. Using a gesture to suggest the unusual length of Pinocchio's nose would be appropriate if you were telling the story about him. The length of his nose is important, and a "repeating" type gesture would help the audience to understand this.

Of course, your nonverbal behavior should not appear stilted and rehearsed during the telling of the story. You want to be natural and make the action *seem* spontaneous and unrehearsed. Suggestions follow for achieving a greater degree of spontaneity as well as for feeling more comfortable as you try to control your nonverbal behavior before your audience.

GESTURES

Gestures should come from the entire body and be a part of it. They should not appear to be something separate, as though their signals were coming from a unique center of their own. To illustrate, if you clench one hand into a fist and pound it into the palm of your other hand, you undoubtedly wish to show anger, strong determination, or some other emotion that may be demonstrated in forceful overt action. For this gesture to be meaningful, not only should there be tension of muscles in the hands but in the arms and throughout the body, accompanied by a facial expression appropriate to the emotion. The most overt action — that is, the pounding with clenched fist — is what the audience sees as action, but that gesture can be effective and evoke the desired emotion only when it emanates from, and is a part of, the body. The "pounding" gesture should be timed to come with what is being said, not before it is said or after.

Hand and arm gestures more than any others tend to give the impression of separateness. Therefore, consider other factors that might help in addition to the "full body accompaniment" recommended for gestures. These suggestions should not be thought of as absolute because exceptions do exist, but in most instances the principles apply.

When a storyteller holds his arms close to his body and bends them only at the elbows or the wrists to gesture, he appears constricted and the gestures seem unnatural. To avoid this, let your arms hang loosely from your shoulders, so that the hand gestures can be made with the whole arm.

In expansive arm and hand gestures, avoid the "stiff arm" effect by using the more natural and pleasing curved line at the elbow. The expansive gestures should be made somewhat to the side instead of straight on. Avoid gestures that come between your face and the audience; go to the side or at least below the face level with them.

When you want to indicate with gestures something that is to the side of you, let's say to the left, gesture with the arm on that side, the left in this case, rather than crossing the body with the right arm.

When you wish to call attention to something you have in your hand, such as a letter, and you gesture as if holding the letter, glance at the letter. The action should be almost simultaneous, the glance slightly preceding the gesture.

TRANSITIONS

Usually there are a few major transitions and many minor ones in a story. They represent "going from one thought to another," and the storyteller should think of them as finishing one thought and starting fresh with another. Transitions require a pause and a "fresh start" with voice and body. The voice and body should be saying, "Don't go away; stay with me. Don't you want to know what happens next?" This should take only a second for minor transitions, longer at major transitions.

At major transitions, move a step or two, or at least definitely shift the weight of your body in a half-step. You may need to work consciously on this movement. Probably all of us have felt glued to the floor at one time or another. Storytellers often say, "My feet wouldn't move; they felt like iron." Just taking a step sounds simple, but for many, the transition movements are the last to be achieved.

If you find it difficult to move your feet in a storytelling situation, try shifting your weight to one foot, leaving the other foot free to step. When we stand, we generally distribute the weight on both feet, with more weight on the balls of the feet than the heels. You cannot lift your foot while weight is on it. Therefore, shift the weight to one foot when you are ready to move. It doesn't matter which foot you step with, if you move directly toward the audience. Most transition movements should take you toward the audience. Sometimes, however, you may want to walk to the side, left or right, either for transition or some other purpose. When you do walk definitely

left or right, or to the side and toward the audience, you should
shift the weight to the foot closest to the audience (that is, the
downstage foot) and lift and step with the foot farthest from the
audience (upstage foot). This principle applies in the same way
to "on stage" walking.

A little practice with this simple procedure followed by
rehearsal in telling the story (with attention to specific transitions) should help you handle transitions.

How to Work for Body Effectiveness

It is easy to say that the body should be free yet attuned to
your will, but to arrive at that happy state while telling the
story is not easily achieved. Some things you can do in practice
sessions that will help prepare you follow.

Exercise

If you exercise regularly, so much the better, because your
general physical condition does affect your performance.
Schedule an exercise session of stretching and relaxing
immediately prior to your rehearsals, particularly at the time
you start working with characterization, and, of course, for all
subsequent rehearsals.

We also recommend exercising just prior to performance.
Although in many situations you may not be able to do stretching exercises before a performance, you may be able to completely relax all your muscles for a moment or two.

Practice

In this preparation step you are focusing attention on all
nonverbal behavior or body language as it concerns your story.
As you approach practice, think "freedom" and "abandon."
Try out many movements and gestures with the words. Some
of them you may be pleased with and decide to keep. Then
practice those particular actions with the words.

You were advised previously to practice movement at transitions. Tell the story now and note what you are doing with transitions. If you are not satisfied with some of them, practice them by taking the steps and shifts as suggested under the topic "Transitions."

Up to this point in your body practice, you have been testing and rehearsing movements and gestures. Now give attention to those occasions in the story when there should be no overt action. As you tell these portions of the story be especially aware of your body behavior. Does your body in its stillness support what is being said? Should it be tensed? Should it be relaxed? It must be attuned to the attitude and mood of the moment in the story.

Now tell the entire story, imagining an audience and visualizing everything as you tell it. Use the movement, gestures, and posture that you have worked on and that seem appropriate. Make the gestures appear spontaneous.

When you finally tell the story for an audience, your body behavior will not be exactly as it was in rehearsal. Some of the action will be repeated, some behavior "on the spot" may be a vast improvement. The total body behavior should be more effective because of your practice.

THE PHYSICAL POSITION OF THE STORYTELLER

Here are several examples taken from true incidents that illustrate the physical position of the storyteller:

A storyteller was asked to tell "Peter Rabbit" during Children's Week in a shopping mall. The site was enclosed, carpeted, and served as a thoroughfare for shoppers. With an audience of approximately two hundred young children seated on the thoroughfare floor, the storyteller used broad actions in characterization and moved among the children at appropriate places — for instance, when looking for the rabbit. He held the audience's attention all the way.

For an adult audience of about fifty, seated at small tables for a luncheon, a storyteller entertained by moving among the tables while telling the story. The tables had been arranged and her "taking of the stage" had been so carefully worked out that she was easily seen by the members of the audience at all times. The objectives for walking among the audience were twofold: first, to highlight the effectiveness of motivated action, and, second, to develop an intimacy with the audience through close physical proximity. There was considerable walking before the story was concluded because the storyteller moved from table to table several times before finishing the story. However, at no time did it seem that the storyteller walked only for the purpose of arriving at a certain place in the room. Every time she moved, some aspect of the story motivated the moving. True, the underlying purpose was to achieve intimate communication with those in the room. Yet the storyteller was so totally lost in the never-never land that moving around the room did not seem contrived. By moving from table to table, the storyteller was able to establish a gracious directness with every member of the audience. Everyone felt included and a part of storyland.

A teacher sat at a table in the corner of her classroom and told a story to a group of eight children, who were sitting around the same table. Later, when the teacher told a story to the entire class of thirty, she stood so that she could be seen easily by all of the children. She started telling the story a few feet away from the children who were seated in the front row so that later she could move in closer to the audience without seeming to be too close, almost on top of the children in the front row.

At a campfire a storyteller hoisted himself up on a box to be a little higher than the others who were sitting and reclining on blankets. As the evening wore on, another member of the group started telling a ghost story from where he sat in half-shadow. He appropriately depended on voice and darkness to create an eerie mood.

Arranged in semicircle on the stage floor, six storytellers sat on pillows and low stools at a storytelling hour for an audience of two hundred. As each storyteller began his story, he moved to the up-center position of the semicircle, thereby including the other storytellers in the audience. During the telling the storyteller moved toward the audience when it seemed appropriate for effective communication.

From the storytelling examples cited above, it is obvious that the physical position a storyteller takes in relation to his or her audience depends on the situation. As in all person-to-person communication, the storyteller should be seen and heard with ease by his audience. At the same time, storytelling seeks an intimacy in communication; folktales in particular call for a down-to-earth, informal atmosphere.

The sitting position of a storyteller with a small audience may create the desired intimacy. When the audience numbers more than fifteen, the storyteller will, in most situations, need to stand in order to be seen and heard. In general, we can say that the larger the audience, the larger should be the projection of both nonverbal and verbal behavior of the storyteller. However, every situation should be considered in light of how one can achieve and maintain intimacy and how well one can be seen and heard.

Most audiences will respond favorably to a storyteller's requests for slight adjustments in arrangement, such as asking people to move closer to the front. Things that clutter the storytelling area, like bulletin boards on wheels or chairs, should be moved. Whether or not they limit the movement of the storyteller or obstruct the view, they may aesthetically bother the audience and the storyteller. Any minor adjustments that will improve the setting and storyteller-audience relationship should be made.

STANDING POSITION

While you are training, stand during most of your storytelling. The standing position permits more freedom of movement and fosters total involvement more than the sitting position does. Once you have learned to tell a story well in the standing position, you will be able to tell it effectively in a sitting position.

CHAPTER SEVEN

Working for Unity and Polish

THE FINAL STEP IN preparing to tell a story is to work for unity and polish, to add the finishing touches, to make the total story a satisfying whole. In this step you should prepare the introductory remarks; attend to the vocabulary, the language style, the time limit; concentrate on the total story; and find a practice audience.

INTRODUCTORY REMARKS

For most storytelling occasions, be prepared to introduce your story with your own introductory remarks. The introduction should acknowledge your right to tell your story to a specific audience. Have material ready for more than one introduction, so that you will be able to adapt the story material to different audiences.

The Nature of an Introduction

Most of the time a few sentences are sufficient to smoothly launch you into the story. One sentence might explain why you chose the story or give some background material for the story, such as its source or cultural setting.

A few examples of introductory remarks follow:

1. Sometimes when we really want something, but have no money to buy it, we daydream and wish someone would give us a whole lot of money. Well, it's never happened to me yet — the receiving, that is — but it did to someone else. . . .

2. When I was a little girl back in Ohio, we always had family gatherings at different relatives' farms. Since I was a "town kid" I really enjoyed the farms. And, boy, the relatives we had! Cousins, uncles, aunts. My favorite relative was my Great Aunt Edith. Edith — sounds very proper, doesn't it? Ha! She was a tough old gal who worked as hard as any of the men on the farm, and could she tell stories! We would all gather around her, and she would talk and talk. She's the one who first got me interested in "endangered species of wildlife." She used to tell us about . . . well, let me tell it in Aunt Edith's own special way. . . .

3. Some of us believe that wishes really come true; and some of us think that that's a lot of nonsense. As for me, I think wishes come true not because of some special omen, but because we have the power ourselves to make it happen. This story, "The Wishing Ring," says what I mean.

4. I love the Christmas season. Something about it affects people in wonderful ways — you see it in their smiles, their eyes, and you feel it in your heart. It makes me think about presents and parties and music and Christmas trees! But not Jaime — he thought about shepherds.

The Title

It is not always necessary to give a title for a story, but when you do, it should be worked into the introductory remarks. Avoid announcing "The title of my story is . . ." This is trite and sounds as though you're going to "recite a piece."

Manner of Communicating Introductory Remarks

Try to establish a friendly relationship with your listeners. Make the introductory comments to the audience direct, communicative, and spontaneous in sound. Keep this intimacy of communication as you go into the story, that is, avoid making a decided break between your introduction and the story itself.

ATTENTION TO VOCABULARY AND SELECTED SENTENCES, PHRASES, REFRAINS

Vocabulary

As you practice telling the whole story, pay some attention to your own language and the language of the author. Are you overusing some words? Check yourself and notice habits that may have developed when you were concentrating on other aspects. You know the story very well now and therefore can make mental notes about the language construction and vocabulary you are using. Ask yourself if what you are doing is appropriate for this story. The author's style of language is more important in some stories than others. For example, local-color stories depend much on language style for their appeal. You may want to check the original story again for style. Are you incorporating enough of the author's vocabulary in your telling?

Selected Sentences, Phrases, and Refrains

You may find an introductory sentence, a particularly well-expressed climax, a concluding sentence, or some other statement or phrase so well stated by the author that you wish to incorporate it in your telling. These should be memorized.

If you are retaining refrains, jingles, or verses in your telling, you undoubtedly memorized them earlier; but check these three items again so there will be no danger of forgetting them when you tell the story.

Time Limit

Time the telling of the story, including your introductory remarks. You will find that the time varies with each telling since the story is not memorized word for word. Check the timing more than once. The time variance in telling is likely to be less than sixty seconds.

If the telling is more than half a minute beyond your time limit, look for some descriptive or minor part that you can leave out. The rate at which you tell the story should be determined by its contribution to the effectiveness of the total story — not because of the time allotted for telling. In other words, don't rush the telling in order to squeeze the story into a given time slot.

Concentration on Total Story

The story you are going to tell becomes as much yours as the author's. You have analyzed the story; you know when to use explanation and description; you know the incidents and how to move the plot along; you know how to suggest characters and have them interact; and you know when to use direct, intimate contact with the audience and when to use other types of contact, Now you must practice with a view to putting it all together.

During this final stage of preparation rehearse in front of a mirror in order to check on your nonverbal behavior. Listen to your voice in order to check on verbal elements. Are you creating the effects you want? If any part of the story needs a change, go back over it — try changes in timing, intensity, quality of voice, and so on.

As you rehearse with full imagination, keep the following items in mind.

1. *Story coherence.* Does the story hang together as a unified whole? Once you catch your listeners up in the story, you don't

want anything to divert them from it. You might think of the story as a dropped ball of yarn that rolls out. The ball may drop, change pace, pick up momentum, slow down, but the yarn should never break. Don't allow the spell of the story to break.

2. *Mood.* Are you establishing the overall mood you want, the mood appropriate for the story?

3. *Transitions.* Are you taking the right amount of time and maintaining interest with a "fresh start" (shifting gears) at the transitions?

4. *Suspense.* As you build toward the highest point of interest, are you involving the audience more and more? Does creating suspense call for a quickening in pace for your story? A decrease in rate? A change in volume? No matter which route you choose for achieving this, it must have been brought about through your personal involvement in developing the suspense of your story.

5. *Climaxes.* Climaxes require emphasis. You may achieve the desired emphasis in different ways. One is an increase in voice intensity (volume); however, the opposite is sometimes more effective — that is, a decrease in volume. Timing is important. You may build suspense with a quickened pace, and then pause before and after the climax. Remember, you have many climaxes that lead to the major one. Note the balance. Do the minor climaxes build appropriately toward the major climax?

6. *Pace, intensity, and projection.* Is the general pace appropriate for your story? Some stories can take a faster rate than others. If you tend to speak rapidly, you will need to be particularly careful to enunciate distinctly in order to be understood easily. Look for the thought-carrying words and give them more time, more care in pronunciation, than others.

Are you using sufficient volume to be heard in an ordinary room? In an effort to create an intimacy of communication, some storytellers drop the volume to a lower level than they realize. One student could hardly believe that she had been speaking in a whisper almost all the way through the story. At certain moments a whisper may be effective, but not for the whole story. Certainly, you want variety of volume in story-telling, but the general intensity should be at a level that is comfortable for the listeners. Take care that very soft utterances may be heard and understood and that very loud utterances do not blast or jar the listeners.

Volume and clarity in pronunciation are not sufficient in themselves to bring about understanding. In fact, excessive volume, as any noise, may obscure what is said. You must *project,* that is "toss out," sounds clearly from the articulators (tongue, teeth, lips) with enough power to reach the back of the room. In working for better projection you might think of the words as Ping-Pong balls being tossed with precision against the back wall. With experience you will learn to adjust the volume and projection of your voice according to different-sized rooms.

A PRACTICE AUDIENCE

This is the time to try your story out on some of your family or close friends. Make it a simple sharing of the story. It's the *story* that you want them to enjoy with you. What are their reactions to it? Never mind about an evaluation of the storyteller.

CHAPTER EIGHT

Anticipating a Real Audience

NOW YOU ARE READY to tell your story to classmates or to some other audience. You have done your work and are thoroughly prepared. Say to yourself, "It ain't no big thing! This is just having fun, letting some other people share my own enjoyment of a story."

Make the telling look easy, spontaneous. Don't try to think of all those details you have worked on. Focus your attention on two things: the story (see it and feel it happen now) and your listeners (let them know you care about them). If you assume that your audience is friendly and you approach it in that way, almost invariably it will be friendly and receptive. Remember, the "story" appeals to human beings the world over. In a way, you're ahead of the game, because the material you are dealing with has interest-catching properties.

As you anticipate an audience, questions may arise such as: What can I do about plain old stage fright? Is it desirable to use props or audiovisual aids in storytelling? What about costuming for storytelling?

STAGE FRIGHT

There is no "cure" for this malady which plagues all of us to some degree at one time or another. Some would say there should not be a cure, since there are desirable as well as undesirable features inherent in the phenomenon. At the moment of stress, and often preceding that moment, the body produces extra adrenalin for meeting a crisis. If the extra energy and alertness can be channeled appropriately into performance, in this case the storytelling, the results are likely to be a more interesting, vibrant performance than if there were no stage fright present.

Although there is no cure, there are some general facts and suggestions for controlling stage fright that may be of some help. First, remember that you have plenty of company; the anxiety or stress commonly called stage fright is a perfectly normal human phenomenon. It is said, "misery loves company."

Second, gain experience. Think of your classroom as the first place to practice. Success breeds success. Successful storytelling experiences will give you confidence. Even so, remember that seasoned professional performers often have stage fright. They, too, have to find ways to control it.

Third, be prepared. Don't short change yourself; take plenty of time to thoroughly study and rehearse.

Fourth, class climate should minimize threats. You are among friends in class, friends who want to enjoy your story and want you to enjoy their stories. You have a common stake in this endeavor as performer and listener. Most instructors do not give ratings for the first round of stories. We strongly subscribe to this principle, since the rating itself may cause fear in some. Evaluation should always emphasize the positive elements, highlighting those features unique in the story and teller. The very nature of the material and procedure in a storytelling class promote a friendly receptive atmosphere. All of these factors should minimize threats from your audience.

Fifth, minimize those threats by counseling yourself, such as, "This isn't life or death. Relax. Enjoy." Sixth, involve yourself in the story, using the extra energy in purposeful action, characterization, and narration. Share your story simply and honestly.

AUDIOVISUAL AIDS

All that is needed for storytelling are the story and the teller. Therefore, anything is possible — any setting, action, or object one could imagine. Storytelling may be combined with other arts, such as puppetry, or a flannel board, or a picture book, or a projection of pictures. These combinations have appeal and may be creative in their own right, but they do not take the place of storytelling, an art that sets no limits on the imagination. Our concern here is with the techniques of what might be called "pure" storytelling. If you develop techniques in storytelling with your own unique talents, you will find it relatively easy to combine storytelling with other arts. For a source treating the combination of storytelling with flannel boards and puppets, see *Storyteller,* by Ramon R. Ross.

There may be occasions when the showing of a picture during the introduction of a story might give information that you consider important to the story. Or a real object, particularly an unusual object, may be shown during an introduction. You should ask yourself whether showing a picture or a real object is really an aid to the total story and if it presents something in a better way than you can paint with words. When you do use aids, it is wise to lay them aside after the introduction and not let them intrude as you carry your listeners into the world of imagination.

We have had students who have successfully used music to create mood, some who have used a guitar as a part of the framework for telling a story, and some who have sung at moments in the telling of a story. If you have the talent and feel secure in doing this, fine; however, we suggest that you make use of this kind of an aid in later presentations instead of the first ones. Obviously when you use music, new factors have to be considered, such as appropriateness, quantity, volume, and so on.

COSTUMING

The storyteller need not think of "costuming" in the same way an actor would, but should think of appropriate attire for every storytelling occasion. A college student was once asked to tell a story to an eighth-grade class in a private school. This was when shorts were common attire on the college campus. The private school, however, had a dress code that barred the wearing of shorts in the classroom. So when the storyteller appeared in her shorts and began telling her story, the eighth graders were so intrigued with what she was wearing that they lost the first part of her story.

Whatever you would feel comfortable wearing while telling a story in front of your peers is acceptable. Often, however, students like to choose something from their wardrobe that is in some way appropriate for their story. One young woman told her story from the point of view of her strong-willed, folksy grandmother, so decided to wear an old-fashioned but also modern long patchwork skirt. It was an excellent choice for it contributed to the atmosphere of the story and was appropriate for both the character-narrator and the college girl.

Another student told "Anatole" with a bit of a French accent and dressed in a modern outfit that could have been seen currently in Paris, New York, or San Francisco. This seemed just right for her. A young man wore his most faded pair of jeans when he told a rugged outdoor adventure story. Another student went still further in creating the atmosphere for a group of children. For the telling of an old folktale of Japan, she chose to wear a traditional Japanese kimono. All of these examples of wearing apparel seemed appropriate for the stories and the storytellers.

Whether you choose to dress with a particular story in mind or not is an individual matter, but always consider what is appropriate for a given audience and occasion.

CHAPTER NINE

Evaluation Chart

THE CHART THAT FOLLOWS may be used for self-evaluation in your preparation and also as a guide in evaluating your peers.

Storytelling Evaluation Chart

Rating Scale: (1) Superior   (3) Good   (5) Poor
                       (2) Excellent   (4) Fair

1. Fluency   _____
2. Communicativeness   _____
3. Visualization   _____
4. Voice   _____
   a. Flexibility
   b. Intensity
   c. Tempo

5. Use of language   _____
   a. Word choice
   b. Language construction
   c. Pronunciation

6. Dramatization (Characterization)   _____

7. Body language   _____
   a. Purposeful?
   b. Well-timed?

8. Suspense   _____

9. Climax   _____

10. General effectiveness   _____
    a. Holding story thread
    b. Audience appeal

Title _____ Summary Rating _____
Name _____ Date _____

My overall rating of this performance is (circle one):
    Superior   Excellent   Good   Fair   Poor

      Evaluator _____

CHAPTER TEN

Story Biography

WE ARE ALL AWARE that a real happening may be stranger and sometimes more interesting than fiction. In fact, fiction itself is generally a reflection of life. Developing a story based on biography is a great challenge for the storyteller. It provides the opportunity for creativity and individuality; it also requires good hard research. Storytellers must be steeped in their subject before they can begin to sift and choose what they will use finally in, say, a ten-minute presentation.

A story based on someone's life is in essence a molding of factual information into story form. The story form will give excitement and drama to the facts. You should not think of story biography as a factual report of someone's life. It is a creative development of a story based on interesting episodes worked into a framework that gives enough information about the person to satisfy the listener.

You may be familiar with longer versions of story biography which have become popular recently in the theater and on television. They are usually labeled as plays or one-man/woman shows; but they more accurately fit the category of story biography. Henry Fonda, for example, played the role of Clarence Darrow, the renowned American trial lawyer. He impersonated Darrow and of course told of his experiences in first person, often speaking directly to the audience. *The Belle of Amherst,* by William Luce, a popular play on Broadway in 1976, starred Julie Harris as poet Emily Dickinson. Through the poet's letters and poems and a storytelling style, a portrait and a partial life story emerges.

Playwright Aldyth Morris used the story biography style for *Damien,* played by Terrance Knapp in Honolulu in 1976. The television production of *Damien* won several awards, including the coveted Peabody Award (1978). Following the *Damien* success Morris used the story biography style with *RLS,* the life of Robert Louis Stevenson, presented as a one-man show by John Davis in Honolulu.

All four of the subjects just mentioned have been treated in shorter story-biographies by students in our storytelling classes. (The analysis paper for the Emily Dickinson story is included at the end of this chapter under "Story Biography Analysis Papers.")

It should be noted that even in the two-hour presentations the life of the subject is, of course, not fully covered. This should make us all the more aware of the limitations set by a ten-minute presentation. It means that some items must be treated in a general fashion, some fleetingly, some skipped, and some in full detail. The final product should have balance in biographical data and episodic detail.

CHOICE OF SUBJECT

The person you choose for a story biography may be living or dead, famous or not. Choosing the subject is a personal matter. Obviously the subject should have some kind of appeal to you. The person may be someone you admire, respect, or love, or someone who incites your curiosity. Many students choose leaders in their own fields of interest and professions — science, art, music, government, sports, religion, education, and others. A teacher chose Julius Caesar as his subject because he intended to use all of his research material and the story itself in classes. (Note the Caesar analysis paper under "Story Biography Analysis Papers.")

Recently a prelaw student was discussing selection possibilities and wondered if a human-interest character story he had found in *Reader's Digest* would be acceptable as a choice. It was pointed out to him that many stories like the one he mentioned do meet most of the criteria for story biography but fail in one important aspect. They rob the student of the valuable process of doing his or her own research and creative development of the story. Since this young man was a debater who intended to study law, it was suggested that he do some reading about the colorful lawyer, Clarence Darrow. This he did and with excellent, quite original results.

If you choose someone who is not well known, the subject should be one with whom you have had some personal connection. One student started her story thus, "The subject of my story is not famous, nor will she ever be. She is my mother." The subject may be a father, grandmother, some other relative, or a close friend. Or the subject might be a colorful family member of the past about whom you have learned through living relatives. Finally, if you wish, you can be your own subject, making the product a story autobiography.

Sources

The phenomenal impact of Alex Haley's bestseller *Roots* has inspired countless numbers of people around the world to delve into their own roots, to search out their own family history. Early in 1977, millions of people sat spellbound at their television sets as they watched the dramatization of *Roots* for eight consecutive nights. It broke all records for television viewing.

According to *Time Magazine,* (February 14, 1977), "Haley learned about his earliest ancestors from an elderly Gambian griot (storyteller), a living repository of oral history who sat him down in the tiny village of Juffure and recited for him the centuries-old saga of his West African clan dating back seven generations to the warrior Kunta Kinte. . . ."

Haley says that the universal appeal of *Roots* is based on "the average American's longing for a sense of heritage." He advocates a three-point plan for cementing family bonds. "I tell young people to go to the oldest members of their family and get as much oral history as possible. Many grandparents carry three or four generations of history in their heads but don't talk about it because they have been ignored. And when the young person starts doing this, the old are warmed to the cockles of their souls and will tell a grandchild everything they can muster."

Secondly, Haley advises the writing of the family history, drawing from the oral history, letters, pictures, news stories, and other memorabilia. Thirdly, he encourages family reunions.

Each of us could probably name one or more friends, relatives, or acquaintances who are following Haley's advice right now. We have one friend who has compiled five thick volumes since *Roots* was televised. Of course, there is nothing new about this activity, but *Roots* served as an impetus in getting many (young and old) started on their family histories.

But why are we giving this much attention to Haley's advice? Simply because if you should choose as your subject a family member or some other personal acquaintance about whom there may not be books, articles, and other printed sources, then the sources mentioned by Haley are for you.

If your subject is not well known to the general public, then your major source is a living person or persons — yourself, relatives, and friends. Additional sources are the family record, personal letters, and other memorabilia as suggested above.

If your subject is a famous person, find books, articles, or news stories. This is the age of memoirs, so there is much material available about famous people, living or dead. It is important that you have more than one source; this gives you more than one point of view and interpretation.

You are fortunate if you can combine written and live sources. In the story of Prince Kuhio, under "Sample Stories Based on Biography," the teller used both sources because the speaker of the story (the friend) was his grandmother. Another storyteller interviewed the widow of Kui Lee, in addition to reading printed accounts of the musician.

POSSIBLE STRUCTURES

Many appealing stories do not follow the simple plot outline listed under the analysis step in this book, and we would not suggest that you be restricted to this pattern. Nevertheless, keep in mind those story elements that maintain interest for an audience as you proceed with the organization of your material. Some suggestions for structure follow:

Introduction

Introductions tend to be longer for biographies than for folktales. You were encouraged to make your introductions to folktales short, but most biographical stories need longer beginnings to meet the criteria of story with plot interest *and* worthwhile information. Often the introduction gives some background of the period and the person, sometimes summarizing accomplishments. The theme, though not usually stated as such, may be made apparent in the introduction.

The flashback technique described earlier is often used to establish a frame for the story. The "Prince Kuhio" storyteller used this device. He told the story from the point of view of the Prince's friend. He briefly gave the setting of the friend's home and family, and an event, a phone call in the middle of the night, "The prince is dead. Won't you come over." The storyteller used the flashback device; he had the friend think back to different incidents in the prince's life as she made her way to the palace. At the palace many objects reminded the friend of important occasions and achievements of Prince Kuhio.

First or Third Person

Biographical stories may be told effectively in the first or third person. If you choose the first-person narration, you will go further in the characterization of the teller than if you were relating the story in the third person. The teller may or may not be the subject of your biography. A young woman chose to tell the story of Anne Boleyn in the first person. She managed to give a sensitive and dramatic characterization of the queen, including, through first person narration, important historical data.

Students more often choose the third-person narration because it generally provides for more objectivity and freedom in treating factual material. In the third-person telling, the point of view is generally that of the storyteller. But you have all of the options for the biography described for other stories under "Analyzing and Adapting the Story." Remember that a story can also be told from a character's point of view in the third person. Such was the case with the Prince Kuhio story. The young man did not wish to impersonate the young woman from whose point of view the story unfolded. Therefore, he said, "She thought about . . ." instead of "I thought about . . ."

One Episode

One episode or event in a person's life may be a story in itself. Add to this an introduction and possibly a conclusion and the story biography will be complete. A simple episode — particularly if the general public is familiar with the person and his or her important achievements — may comprise the meat of a story. Such is the case with the Lincoln story, "Why Lincoln Grew a Beard," which you will find under "Sample Stories Based on Biography." As the storyteller says, it is "an intimate portrait of Abe Lincoln as seen by a little eleven-year-old girl who suggested in a letter that he grow the famous beard." In her introduction the storyteller reminds us that many stories have been told about the sixteenth president of the United States. She lists several of those major story topics, gives us a character and physical description, particularly as viewed by children, and leads into the story. No concluding remarks by the storyteller are needed in this instance.

More often, if only one episode is chosen for the biography story, it will be a major event. For example, one student chose to focus on the execution of Marie Antoinette, but she preceded this telling with some general historical background.

Several Episodes

There are many ways to use several important events as a story. One popular way is chronological order, treating certain periods of a life as they happen in time. One student built her story around three important episodes in the life of Helen Keller, starting with her youth. Each episode projected the theme of great determination and perseverance on the part of Helen Keller when confronted with seemingly insurmountable obstacles.

A certain period of a life may be treated chronologically, emphasizing the major events of that period. Note the Julius Caesar outline referred to earlier; it is concerned with Caesar's rise to power and fall.

Finally, several episodes may be used without following chronological order.

Portraits and Philosophy

Although we encourage you to play up happenings in biography, there are fine story biographies that emphasize the character and philosophy of the subject more than life events. The Emily Dickinson story is an example of this treatment. We learn about Dickinson through her poetry. Kui Lee has been the subject of many story biographies. In one instance, the storyteller developed the story around Lee's love for his wife and for Hawaii. Along with the narrative, the storyteller quoted from and sang Lee's songs, which depicted these concepts.

Conclusions

Conclusions of story biographies can vary a great deal. Whereas earlier you were warned that long conclusions could detract from the overall appeal of a story, some biographical stories need long conclusions. For instance, if you have emphasized one early period of someone's life for your story, you may make the total presentation stronger by concluding with a summary of major achievements that followed the period of story concentration. Look at and consider effective endings of short stories and folklore employed by different authors. All of these options are open to you.

An example of a surprise ending to a story biography comes to mind. Although we heard the story many years ago, the climax and conclusion are still vivid. The story started with the arrival in Hawaii of the storyteller's great grandfather as a young immigrant from Japan. It proceeded to tell of his hardships due to the language barrier and differences in culture, as well as to his difficulty in finding jobs. It built to a period of unusual depression for the young man; his wife died, leaving him with three small children.

One evening, in a weak moment when he felt there was no way he could support the children or take care of them, he decided to end his own life and theirs. He went to the kitchen and took a large butcher knife from the drawer. The children were asleep in one room. First, he went to the baby's crib. He raised the knife over the baby, but at that moment ashes floated down and settled on the blade.

He looked up and realized that they had come from the urn sitting on a high shelf above the crib. They were the ashes of his wife. This happening brought him to his senses. He walked back to the kitchen and slammed the knife into the drawer: "Never, never again will I allow such thoughts to come!"

And of course he didn't, as the storyteller pointed out, "else he wouldn't be ninety-three today, and I wouldn't be here at all."

PRESENTATION

Up to now you have been concerned with the choice of a subject, the research, and the organizing of material. In the process you have created a story biography script. Since you are the author of this work, the analysis has taken place concurrently with the development of the story.

The analysis paper is basically like other story analysis papers: title, sources (usually longer), statement of theme, description of at least the major story personality, and outline of what you will include. Labeling the initial incident, plot development, climax, and conclusion is also recommended.

In preparing for presentation, proceed with the system presented in part one, concentrating on fluency, characterization, bodily action and control, visualization, and unity and polish. Minor modifications under fluency and characterization should be pointed out. The fluency step should be taken in preparing story biography, as with other stories, to learn the sequence of events and to develop a flow of language. In the actual presentation, however, you may refer to brief notes if you wish. Whereas all other stories should be told without notes or scripts of any kind, it is appropriate to use notes for some stories based on fact. In general it is preferable to arrange the notes on cards. However, letters and other quotations may be read from a book if this seems more fitting.

The storyteller of the Marie Antoinette biography held a scroll in her hand until she was ready to read a letter. Then she unrolled the scroll and read the message. This was appropriate for the subject and was the only time the storyteller used notes. Avoid using large sheets of paper. The notes may indicate transitions, dates, quotations, and the like. A warning: do not let the notes become a crutch — do not be bound to them. To use or not to use notes in presenting a story biography is *your* option.

What about characterization in the story biography? Understanding characters and projecting that understanding is important. But having characters speak to each other is optional. Character portrayal here is not as important as in some stories — that is, it is not necessary that you "sound like" or "look like" that person. Neither is characterization ruled out for those who can make their presentations more effective by using it. Few will attempt to impersonate their subjects, using instead attitude, language, and imagery to create a vivid picture of the subject.

Give yourself plenty of time for oral practice when you have finished the analysis step and prepared your script. Go on with the other preparation steps so that you can hold the attention of your audience with story biography as much as with any tale of fiction.

Conclusion

But something marvelous happened between that session and his telling of the story for the class. From the moment he appeared and started with his first words, the story began to unfold. The boy was totally involved with the telling — no longer was he just relating incidents — he was personally re-living them. He had entered never-never land and taken us with him.

MANY TIMES ONE'S PATH unexpectedly crosses that of an acquaintance of yesteryear. It was our good fortune to be a part of an intimate situation with this same boy some twelve years after he told the story in class. The occasion was a prewedding dinner. He was the best man for a good friend. The dinner per usual was profusely colored with the friendly and at times raucous banter of such occasions.

During a lull in the facetious remarks, the best man rose to present a toast to the groom. As he stood, a picture of the boy who used to stand in front of the class so unemotionally and uninvolved came to mind. But that picture soon faded for in front of us was a young man who was fluent, sincere, and completely poised as he related some of the incidents of his relationship with the groom during their schooldays. The mood was immediately changed from that of frivolous banter to serious and respectful meditation when the young man recalled some of his most meaningful associations with the groom. The young man was not just relating incidents — he was personally reliving them, and this personal involvement motivated us, the members of his audience, to relive these experiences with him.

Many, many pictures of former storytelling students flash before us. Some of them are following careers in the performing arts, but many more are in such diverse professions as education, medicine, law, business, engineering, journalism, religion, and homemaking.

Storytelling is for everybody. Some will pursue it as a highly developed performing art and become true artists of storytelling; others will use the storytelling craft as an aid in reaching professional goals. All who seriously study and participate in storytelling will receive personal satisfaction and growth in the process. We invite you to discover resources of imagination and aesthetic enjoyment in yourself, to discover your own connection with the continuum of human tradition and experience. We hope you will discover the sheer joy of communicating a story, a feeling of oneness with your audience, be it great or small. When that moment of oneness arrives, the hours of searching for a story, analyzing it, working for fluency, characterization, visualization, bodily action and control, unity, and polish will seem time well spent.

Selected Samples
for the Storyteller

THE FOLLOWING STORIES, "WHY Lincoln Grew a Beard," "Prince Kuhio," and "Haha," were prepared and told by students in storytelling classes at the University of Hawaii.

Why Lincoln Grew a Beard

by Hideko Asou

Many stories have been told about Abe Lincoln, the sixteenth president of the United States of America, about his early life as a pioneer child on a Kentucky farm, about his career as a captain in the Black Hawk War, as a lawyer, as a Republican candidate, as the president who held the nation together during the Civil War, and, yes, stories about his tragic assassination.

He appears before us as "Honest Abe," as brave Abe, as a man of decision, as a man with intense humanity, and as a good and close friend of the "plain common people" and their children.

Possibly no other president has ever been loved so much by children. To them he was like something out of a picture book. So tall, so bony, so quizzical, and so comic — he was the Strange Friend and he was the Friendly Stranger. He met the eye as a clumsy, mystical giant that had walked out of a Chinese or Russian fairy story or a bogey, who had stumbled out of an ancient Saxon myth with a big handkerchief full of presents he wanted to divide among all the children in the world. And Abe Lincoln did give priceless gifts to all the children he met. Lincoln's great love for children always won their confidence. Wherever he went, he was surrounded by those little friends who loved him so much and whom he loved as his own children.

Here is a warm and intimate portrait of Abe Lincoln as seen by a little eleven-year-old girl, who suggested in a letter that he grow the famous beard. Abe Lincoln himself enjoyed telling this story very, very much.

It was one October evening in 1860. The place, Westfield in New York State. Grace Bedell, an eleven-year-old girl, sat in her attic room looking at a picture which her father had given her. It was not a drawing and it was not a painting; yet you could see every hair on Lincoln's head and all the details of his clothing. It was the first photograph Grace had ever seen. It gave her a strange feeling that the tall, lean man himself was looking at her.

Grace's little lamp threw shadows on the black-and-white photograph. The features seemed to come alive. A series of small shadows lay around the thin face and covered the hollow cheeks. "Whiskers!" she thought.

"How *becoming!*" she said to herself. "Somebody should tell him. If he really had whiskers, all the ladies would like him. They would ask their husbands to vote for him, and he would become president. I must tell him."

She reached for a pen and began to write a letter:

Mr. Abraham Lincoln

Dear Sir:

I am a little girl, eleven years old, but I want you to be President of the United States very much. So I hope you won't think me very bold to write to such a great man as you are.

Have you a little girl about as large as I am? If so, give her my love and tell her to write me if you cannot answer this letter. I have four brothers and some of them will vote for you. If you will let your whiskers grow, I will try to get the others to vote for you. You would look a good deal better, for your face is so thin. All the ladies like whiskers, and they would ask their husbands to vote for you. Then you would become President.

Grace Bedell

At that time about fifty letters a day arrived at the Lincoln campaign headquarters. Lincoln saw only those from friends and from very important people. His two secretaries, John Nicolay and John Hay, considered all other mail unimportant and usually did not give it to Lincoln.

Grace's letter was picked up by John Hay, and he was very much interested in her original idea. But John Nicolay was not impressed and suggested that Grace's letter be tossed into the wastebasket. They began arguing and neither of them would give in.

Just then Mr. Lincoln walked through the door. Now, Abe Lincoln loved little girls. Whenever he met one on the street, he would always stop to talk to her. There was no reason for him to throw a letter from a little girl into the wastebasket. He took the letter and began to read it. A delighted smile came upon his face.

A few days later Grace received this letter from Springfield, Illinois:

My dear little Miss,

Your very agreeable letter of October 15th has been received. I regret the necessity of saying that I have no daughters. But I have three sons: one seventeen, one nine, and one seven years of age. They, with their mother, constitute my entire family.

As to the whiskers, having never worn any, do you not think people would call it a piece of silly affectation if I were to begin now?

Your very sincere well-wisher,

A. Lincoln

I believe you could imagine what a pleasant thrill of excitement this young girl experienced when she read this letter.

On February sixteenth of the following year a special train carried the newly elected President Lincoln from Illinois to the White House. The people of Westfield learned that the train would stop briefly at a station near their town. The Bedell family, too, heard the news, and they went to the station. They found a large sign with the words "Hail to the Chief" above the tracks and the Stars and Stripes flying from the roof of the station.

As Grace looked around at the many strange faces, there was a sudden silence. A thousand ears strained to listen. "Here comes the train!" someone in the crowd shouted.

Grace raised her eyes as high as she could and saw the top of a black railway engine pass slowly beyond the heads of the people in front of her. Then came the flat roof of a railway car, and another, and a third with the Stars and Stripes waving from the back of it.

A very tall, black hat stood a little higher than a lot of other black hats — that was all Grace could see. Some of the people were shouting, "Speech! Speech!" and Grace held her breath. All around her everyone became quiet.

"Ladies and gentlemen," someone said, "I have no speech to make and no time to make it. I appear before you so that I may see you and you may see me."

Grace felt ice-cold. It was *he* — his voice. *He* was up there on the platform. She tried hard to see him, but all she could see was the black hat.

Lincoln was speaking again. "I have but one question, standing here beside the flag: Will you give me the support a man needs to be president of our country?"

Hands and hats rose into the air along with loud voices: "Yes — yes — we certainly will, Abe!"

Once more Grace heard Lincoln. "I have a little correspondent in this place," he said. "This little lady told me how to improve my appearance, and I want to thank her. If she is present, I would like to speak to her."

"Tell us her name," someone shouted. "The name!"

And Lincoln replied: "Her name is Grace Bedell."

Her father took Grace's hand and led her forward. People around opened a path for them, whispering and pointing at them with their fingers. She went to the one who had asked for her by name.

Her father lifted her up to the platform in sight of a thousand people, up to a pair of big feet.

Somewhere above her she heard a slow chuckle. "She wrote to me that she thought I would look better if I wore whiskers."

He stopped. Grace felt strong hands under her arms. Then, as if she had no weight at all, she was raised high in the air, kissed on both cheeks and gently set down again.

Now, she forgot all about the people. Grace looked up and laughed happily, for up there on the rugged face she saw the whiskers. "You see, I let them grow just for you, Grace," said Lincoln.

Grace could do nothing but look at the tall, plain, great man. She would have been happy to stand and look forever and ever.

Then Lincoln took her hand, and she heard him say, "I hope to see you again, my little friend, sometime." Then she understood that this moment had to end. He helped her down the steps of the railway car, and Grace went obediently, like a good girl, back to her proud father.

Grace heard the train whistle and the loud noise of the engine starting again on its journey. People cheered and waved after the train until it was far down the tracks. But in her mind Grace heard only three words repeated over and over again: "My little friend."

Prince Kuhio

by Woody Fern

Prince Jonah Kuhio Kalanianaole — Friday, January 6, 1922!

Uluniu and Koa Avenues are in the heart of Pualeilani, the district of Waikiki. Mrs. Harriet Peterson sat on her porch, which borders both these streets. It was early evening and the winter's sun was slowly setting in the western sky. David Peterson came up the street carrying his ever-present brief case and looking very tired. He'd just come from the streetcar, the same streetcar he boarded at seven this morning, and here it was six in the evening. Harriet welcomed her husband. The family sat down for the evening meal and all were unusually quiet that night, all except two-month-old Nani. The rest of the family retired early, for all were bushed from hard work and play that day — all except Nani. Harriet finally rocked Nani to sleep and put her in her crib. And about 10:00 P.M., Harriet herself was able to climb into bed to begin what was destined to be a short and much troubled rest.

At about 2:45 A.M., the phone began to ring. At first Harriet thought it was a dream; but it was persistent — ring, ring, ring! Harriet staggered out of bed and sleepily walked down the hall. She was apprehensive as she went to the telephone, for a call at this time of night would either be the wrong number or bad news.

"Hello? Hello?"

"Harriet, this is Kahanu. The prince is dead. Won't you come over?"

Harriet was stunned. She could hardly speak. Finally she gathered herself and said, "Yes, I'll be right there."

Even in strenuous times a mother's instincts seem to make her care for her own first. Harriet ran next door and awoke Mrs. Sherlock, asking her to watch the young baby, Nani. As she readied herself, Harriet couldn't help but think of the little child — the first one born in Waikiki, the one they'd name Naniopualeilani, the beauty of Pualeilani. Pualeilani had been the home of Queen Kapiolani. And then Waikiki was subdivided. And she remembered the prince, presenting them with a calabash bowl as the first landowners in all of Royal Grove. Harriet was ready now as she left by the side door and walked down the driveway.

In the moonlight she could see at the end of the driveway two royal palm trees — these had graced Pualeilani, when Queen Kapiolani had lived there. She headed down toward another Pualeilani — the palace that the prince and Kahanu had built right on the beach, a castle if there ever was one. As she was walking down the street, Harriet began to cry, and she was ashamed of herself, for she was a strong-willed woman. She tried to think about Kuhio's life, and she did. She remembered her aunt telling her about the time Kuhio was a political prisoner and how he became engaged to Kahanu while in prison. All he had tried to do was to help Liliuokalani regain her throne, but they had failed.

And then she remembered the sporting events that the prince participated in and supervised — the football games at Punahou, the sailing and rowing races in Honolulu harbor. Yes, and even the golf matches with the visiting dignitaries. Oh, many of these were pictured in the *Honolulu Advertiser* sports section and on the front page. And then his ten terms of territorial delegate to Congress from Hawaii. His long record of achievements — Hansen's disease settlement at Kalaupapa, development of Pearl Harbor, and his speech: "While Hawaii stands, our coastline down the long way to the Panama Canal zone from Alaska is safe from successful invasion or attack." Yes, Kuhio had even gone to see President Teddy Roosevelt — about Pearl Harbor, developing the harbors and buildings, women's suffrage.

Yes, Kuhio loved the Hawaiian people. They were his people. He felt they were being corrupted by city life. He was eloquent when he spoke to the House and Senate in Washington, telling them of his people — how he wanted to get his people back to their land, to live on and work on — the native Hawaiian, the indigenous people of Hawaii, a dying race. His efforts culminated in the Rehabilitation Act of 1921, which eventually became known as the Hawaiian Homes Commission Act. And now, the champion is gone.

Harriet entered the house, and as she did she saw the vases filled with silverswords. Oh yes, the twenty-fifth wedding anniversary of Kahanu and Kuhio. October 8, just last year, the dancing platform — Kahanu in white, with her silver tiara and silver fan, and the prince in his white dinner jacket with the red ribbon across his chest, upon which was affixed the emblem of the Order of Kapiolani. And the pier out onto the water upon which all the tables were set for the guests.

One of the servants met Harriet and took her upstairs to the bedroom where the now-still prince lay dead. She couldn't remember the prince in this way. She had to remember him as she always had. She remembered him calling to her in Hawaiian from her back porch — and teasing — "Eh, Hattie! How's the beauty of Waikiki?" And yet she had teased him, too — "Go away, you old goat!" And now he is gone.

The prince wanted a simple funeral, but the Hawaiians wouldn't have it. After all he was the last of the line, the last of the royal heroes of the King Kamehameha and King Kalakaua dynasties. His body lay in state first at Kawaiahao Church and then at Iolani Palace. Every hour there was a change of watch of Kuhio's body. Then the casket was taken up Nuuanu Pali and interred — the last of the line. And Harriet, like many of the Hawaiians and haoles alike, was sad. But life goes on. So it has, for you see, Harriet was my grandmother, and David is my grandfather, and Naniopualeilani is my mother.

Haha (My Mother)

by Kay Ishimoto

The person whose story I am about to relate is not famous nor will she ever be, for that person is my mother.

I always thought of my mother as being a rather cold and unloving person. As a child I found lots of proof. Where other mothers often hugged and kissed their children, as far back as

I could remember, my mother never touched me or my younger brothers in affection. Other mothers often walked their children to school holding their hands. My mother had me taking my brother to school instead. Then of course when children were leaving home for trips and such, I had heard their mothers say things like "Mother will miss you!" or "Mama loves you, now. Hurry home." Instead, my mother never set a curfew, and whenever I left home her words were always the same, "Yasai wo wasurenai de tabenasai yo," which meant, "Don't forget to eat your vegetables."

In the summer of 1970 I left my mother at home in Honolulu and went to Japan for a visit. My grandmother (in Japan) gave me more details of Mother's life — some I'd known before, some I'd not. But together they combined to form the pieces for an understanding that I had not been able to find before.

Mother was born Hiroko Ouchi in 1929 in a Soto Shu temple on the island of Molokai to Soshun and Tsuneko Ouchi. Her father had been working as a Zen missionary with Father Danton, who was continuing the work of Father Damien.

After a while Mother began using more English than Japanese and so did her younger sisters. Her father felt she was forgetting her Japanese heritage and moved the whole family back to Japan and then later to Korea. Mother was five at the time. In Korea, Soshun Ouchi set up a school for learning. Mother was the top student right up to the time of the war.

Japan was losing the war and rather than "lose face," they began to send older men as well as priests off to help fight or work for the war. Mother was sixteen when her father was sent to Siberia to work in the trenches. He was captured by the Russians there and subjected to endless torturing and brainwashing techniques, which miraculously he survived. While this was going on, Mother, her mother, two sisters, and a brother had to escape from Korea into Japan. Mother, being the eldest child, had to assume her father's calm and perseverance. Survival relied often on keeping a closed heart. Often their rations consisted of beetles and grass and locusts. All along their escape route they saw mountains of bodies of people who had died from the winter and starvation. One had to really shut his heart or he would be running to every child's voice crying in the snow and there were just too many cries. Mother's baby brother died on this trip. There were also too many times when mothers had to still their own babies with death so that the people's hiding place would not be discovered. Whenever Mother speaks of the war, the sadness of the knowledge of what tragedies men can do to each other is etched upon her face.

After Grandfather got back from Siberia he immediately made plans to have Mother come to Hawaii to marry a man she had never met before. Mother was, in fact, in love with and about to marry another man at the time. But Grandfather felt that she could not stay in a country of defeat. There was no questioning, only obedience, for that was the Japanese way. Mother in true Japanese fashion carried out her father's orders stoically.

I had known about these orders and thus expected to find my grandfather a cold, meditative, stoic, and probably a brilliant man. I was right. After a quiet breakfast, Grandfather often lectured me on being strong and keeping my mind a free spirit. I was to learn to keep my emotions from blocking growth. He also hinted very, very strongly that I should keep up my studies in speaking Japanese. One of the hardest things, though, to get used to was that he very rarely smiled.

One morning, after the lecture session, Grandfather left for his study, and Grandmother and I sat over our last cup of coffee. "Your mother misses you, Natsuko," she said.

"Oh, no, Grandmother," I said, "Mother is really a stoic, and I'm sure she doesn't feel anything."

Suddenly she got up and went into her room. In a moment she came back with a letter. The letter read, "Mama mo Kay ga hikooki ni notte sora no mukoo ni mienaku naru made tatteru node Dennis ni mama wa Kay ga nihon ni tsuku made tatteru no, to wararemashita." The translation is, "After Kay boarded the plane I watched it as it began to disappear into the far off sky until her brother laughingly said, 'Mama, are you going to watch until it reaches Japan?' "

Grandmother then passed the letter for me to look at and my eyes were drawn to the last line, which mother had meant for me. "Sooshite yasai wo wasurenai de tabesashite kudasai." ["Don't forget to eat your vegetables."] It took a good deal of control to keep my tears from falling into my coffee.

"You see," Grandmother began, "the Japanese mother is like a lion's mother. A lion's mother will throw her cubs off a hill, and the one that survives is the one she nurtures. It may seem cruel, but in a country such as Japan where the land is small and competition is keen, mothers must have their children able to survive with honor and dignity." It was at this point that all those pieces I had begun to find began to jell.

My last night was spent in Tokyo. It was about eight-thirty at night when the telephone ring shattered the silence of the cubicle that was my hotel room. I spoke to all my relatives, and they all wished me a happy journey. Suddenly a familiar strong and clear voice sounded on the line, "Natsuko, are you all right in Tokyo? Be careful not to go out at night, it's dangerous."

"Hai," I answered.

"Don't forget to study your Japanese. It is important."

"Hai."

Then there was a pause and the silence seemed to draw down on me, and then suddenly clear and strong and stoic as ever,

"Sooshite, Natsuko, yasai wo wasurenai de tabenasai yo."
["Don't forget to eat your vegetables."]

"Hai," I stammered.

"Sayoonara."

"Goodbye."

The line went dead then. I stood with the receiver in my hand not knowing what to think or do. Then I remembered. I looked outside my small window to the lights of Tokyo that seemed to be glowing a little like Christmas tree lights. I slowly put the receiver back onto the hook and smiled.

STORY BIOGRAPHY ANALYSIS PAPERS

The three analyses of story biographies included in this section were prepared by students in University of Hawaii classes. They follow the format described earlier.

1. Story Biography Analysis

by Harry Tindall

I. *Title:*
   Julius Caesar

II. *Authors and Sources:*
   Duggan, Alfred, *Julius Caesar: A Great Life in Brief,* Alfred A. Knopf, New York, 1966.

   Ferrero Guglielmo, *The Life of Caesar,* G. P. Putnam and Sons, New York, 1933.

   Fuller, J. F. C., *Julius Caesar,* Rutgers University Press, New Brunswick, N. J., 1965.

   Komroff, Manuel, *Julius Caesar,* Julian Messner, New York, 1955.

III. *Characters:*
   Julius Caesar — An aristocrat and universal genius, at once a student, artist, man of action, with soaring but

practical imagination, balanced intelligence, untiring
energy, lightning quickness of decision, elastic control of temper, iron self-control but indifference to
sentiment — an opportunist.

Pompey the Great — Brilliant Roman general who never
understood the political intrigue so necessary to holding power.

Vercingetorix — Military and spiritual leader of the
Gauls in their fight against Caesar.

IV. *Theme:*

Genius, untempered by understanding and compas-
sion, can arouse unreasoned hatred and jealousy in
fellow men.

V. *Introduction:*

"Cowards die many times before their deaths;
The valiant never taste of death but once.
Of all the wonders that I yet have heard,
It seems to me most strange that men should fear;
Seeing that death, a necessary end,
Will come when it will come."

So spoke Caesar in Shakespeare's *Julius Caesar* and
thereby put the finger on one of the two attributes that
drove the greatest Roman of them all to unparalleled
success — and sudden, tragic death.

VI. *Initial Incident:*

Caesar was born an aristocrat on the wrong side of the
political fence, a nephew and disciple of Marius, Man of
the People.

VII. *Incidents:*

A. Young Caesar bucks Dictator Sulla but manages to
survive.

B. Caesar, captured by pirates, not only survives but
crucifies them all after his release.

C. Caesar recruits army and holds off barbarians in Asia Minor.

D. Caesar climbs political ladder to highest office in Rome.

E. Caesar scales military heights in Britain, Gaul, and Germany.

F. Caesar challenges Pompey and Roman Senate, wins in Spain, Greece, Egypt.

G. Caesar is made dictator of Rome for life, but jealousy and hatred mount.

H. Caesar is assassinated in Senate. (Climax)

I. Long civil war ensues and ends with Caesar's heir gaining power. Empire flourishes for two-hundred years. (Conclusion)

2. Story Biography Analysis

by Sherry Munger

I. *Title:*

Judge Tenderly of Me

II. *Sources:*

Bradley, Edward Sculley, et al., *The American Tradition in Literature,* Vol. 2. W. W. Norton and Company, Inc., New York, 1967.

MacLeish, Archibald, et al., *Emily Dickinson: Three Views,* Amherst College Press, Amherst, Mass., 1960.

Scott, Winfield T., ed., *Judge Tenderly of Me: The Poems of Emily Dickinson,* Hallmark Cards, Inc., Kansas City, Mo., 1968.

Sherwood, William R., *Circumference and Circumstances: Stages in the Mind and Art of Emily Dickinson,* Columbia University Press, New York, 1968.

Taggard, Genevieve, *The Life and Mind of Emily Dickinson,* Cooper Square Publishers, Inc., New York, 1967.

Todd, Mabel Loomis, ed., *Letters of Emily Dickinson,* World Publishing Company, Cleveland, New York, 1951.

III. *Characters:*

Emily Dickinson — The main character, of course, is Emily Dickinson, who was a complex person, sensitive to life and death, joy and sorrow, hate, fear, and love, and one who had the artful ability to immortalize these feelings in words of poetry.

William Austin Dickinson — Emily's brother and early confidant.

Levinia (Vinnie) Dickinson — Emily's younger sister.

IV. *Theme:*

Below the surface of Emily Dickinson there was a personality full of sparkling humor and in constant communication with nature.

V. *Introduction:*

Since Emily Dickinson was published (except for seven poems) only after her death, the only record of her inner feelings we have are her letters and poetry. Most people are familiar only with the latter, and because a wealth of her poetry deals with death and immortality (a very common topic in the days she was writing) many tend to judge her as an overly morbid soul who lived the secluded life of a recluse.

VI. *Story Sequence:*

1. This is not true, for her seclusion was not even near total, and one may look at her other poems and see the identification with things other than death or sadness.

2. Biographical material — Born 1830; attended Amherst Academy 1846; father died and left her with

mother, who was, soon after, paralyzed; much contro-
versy over whether she did or did not fall in love
(romantically) several different times in her life. Two
years before her death at age fifty-five, she suffered a
stroke and was thereafter a semi-invalid.

3. She did not take her seclusion seriously, as evidenced
   in a letter to her brother while she was in Amherst
   (read part of letter).

4. Her nature poetry reflects her witty and humorous
   attitude toward much in life (poem "I'm Nobody").
   Her love of the sensual beauty of nature is exemplified
   by "I Taste a Liquor Never Brewed" (read poem).

5. "The soul selects her own society — then shuts the
   door," but fortunately through her poems and letters,
   we find a blessed little opening in that door. (Climax)

VII. *Conclusion:*

Emily Dickinson, a very complicated person — those
of us who see the majesty of her poetry listen intently to
her plea, "This is my letter to the World/The simple
news that nature told/For love of her/Judge tenderly
of me."

3. Story Biography Analysis

by Kenneth M. Ono

I. *Title:*

Not Lucky Come Hawaii

II. *Author:*

Kenneth M. Ono

III. *Sources:*

Interview with subject himself. Interviews with three of
his daughters.

IV. *Theme:*

Not lucky come Hawaii, but Hawaii mo' bettah.

V. *Description of Subject of Biography:*

He is an old man, Japanese like me. His first name is Matsu. His last name is unimportant for he has done nothing in his lifetime that can be considered uniquely or historically memorable and monumental. He is not famous. His physical structure is relatively large for a Japanese: he is broad-shouldered and heavy-boned, but lean. Covering his body are baggy, worn-out khaki trousers and a loose, faded aloha shirt — both bleached by age. His exposed arms, neck, and head reveal skin tanned a permanent brown. The skin is wrinkled all over save the top of his head, which is smooth and shining because the hairs there are very few and far between. Upon a rather slender oval face and below a high forehead is a remarkably high-bridged nose. On this almost-Roman nose rests a pair of, not thick, but thin glasses through which his dark brown eyes shine sharply.

He is the first generation of Japanese to come to Hawaii. He is my grandfather. All his grandchildren call him "Jiji" (equivalent to "Grandpa" in English).

VI. *Structure of Biography:*

It was right here in Honolulu, Hawaii. The day and date is Sunday, November 8, 1970. (It will be nine days ago when I tell this biography on November 17.) It is a typically peaceful and quiet Sunday morning. The weather is fine: the sun is warm, fluffy bunches of white clouds are scattered here and there upon a bright blue sky. I personally have come to this house and its patio, which overlooks Moanalua Gardens, Lunalilo Freeway, Gibson's Discount Store, Sand Island, and on out to the sea's horizon. There is a comfortable breeze blowing down from the hills of Tripler Army Hospital. Here he is! Right here in this patio. I have come to interview him, to get from him the facts of his life (description of subject).

VII. *Introduction:*

I am Sansei, third-generation Japanese. He is Issei, first-generation Japanese. He speaks primarily Japanese; I do not. But I have brought along a competent and appropriate translator: a Nisei, a second-generation Japanese, my mother and his daughter.

We all sit down at a picnic table, I opposite the old man and my translator. I explain the reason for my interrogating him; my translator translates. He nods consent and smiles, finding it amusing.

VIII. *Initial Incident:*

To begin, I ask for initial impersonal, formal facts: name, date of birth, age, education, etc. His answers are distinct; his pronunciation precise; his speech is steady, smooth, and fluent. I do not understand until his Japanese is translated. He says, in Japanese, his name is Matsu. It means tall pine tree — a fitting name, for he was once 5 feet 11 inches tall (pretty tall for a Japanese), but age has bent him to a shorter 5 feet 6 inches. Date of birth: May 21, 1891. Age: eighty — eighty? Oh yes, correct according to the traditional Japanese accounting of your age; you are already a year old the day you're born. Education: eight years.

IX. *Plot Development:*

I ask about his immigration to Hawaii. In Japanese he relates his entire past, beginning with his arrival here in Hawaii. His memory is excellent at the age of eighty! He arrived at Pier 2, Honolulu Harbor, on July 26, 1906, on board the no-longer-existing ship *Manchuria*. He was fifteen years old with no friends or relations here.

He pours forth the facts of his life, incessantly, and they seem to pile up into infinity. My translator translates as fast as she can. I do not want to interrupt him, and I give up taking notes.

While recalling his past he holds a fly swatter in his right hand. An occasional fly lands on the picnic table, he cracks it and sweeps it off the table agilely.

At the end of 1920 he moved to Honolulu permanently and labored as a stevedore . . . he was injured by a ship's boom in 1939 and almost killed, but a year of hospitalization and rehabilitation helps him overcome one crisis only to encounter another — World War II.

War is a bad thing, he says. Japanese planes attacked Pearl Harbor. He is Japanese, but with two sons in the U. S. Army he hopes America wins. He smiles — the war ended and his two sons returned.

Has he become a naturalized American citizen? No.

Does this first-generation Japanese, a Japanese alien, prefer Japan over Hawaii? Of course, he prefers the fortunate life-style in Hawaii.

Ah! Then Hawaii has been fortunate for you, "Jiji!" Lucky Come Hawaii!

X. *Climax:*

My translator translates, *not* lucky come Hawaii. He looks at me and scolds, "Baka-tare!" (the English equivalent is stupid or silly fool). Then he says to me in his best broken, pidgin English with a Japanese accent, "Hawaii mo' bettah!" I understand: he did not become famous or wealthy. He is even now displeased with his monthly Social Security check, a measly $175. Not "lucky come Hawaii," but "Hawaii mo' bettah."

XI. *Conclusion:*

A voice announces lunch. The morning is spent, filled with facts and feelings of Jiji's past. It's five minutes of noon. We go into the kitchen to eat. I'm not hungry. I watch Jiji sit in a chair at the table and eat with a fork. He finishes, washes lunch down with Japanese tea. I prepare to leave. I say goodbye and hope to see you soon. Well, I don't know how to conclude because there is no conclusion. Jiji is alive and well and enjoying life in Hawaii.

SELECTED STORIES

John Henry[1]

John Henry was a steel-drivin' man: famous Negro strong man and work hero, known and talked about and bragged about and yarned about and sung about in every Negro work camp, construction gang, and levee camp in the South. And he died with his hammer in his hand: the twelve-pound hammer (some say twenty) that flashed like gold when he swung it. The women used to come out from town where John Henry worked to hear John Henry sing and the hammer ring.

John Henry was probably a real person, but so much legend has grown up around his prowess that it is hard to be sure. He was born in Tennessee (Mississippi also claims the honor) and was thirty-four years old when he died. He was a big man — 220 pounds.

The John Henry story begins in the early 1870s, when the Big Bend Tunnel of the Chesapeake and Ohio Railroad was being built nine miles east of Hilton in the West Virginia hills. John Henry had prodigious strength and a prodigious work record. He could drive steel ten hours without stopping. He could drive his drill into solid rock and shake down mountains. They say he took sick one day, and his wife went to work in his place: pretty Polly Ann, drivin' steel like a man. (Some say her name was Lucy Ann, and some say Pauline.)

One day the boss bought a steam drill to hurry the work in the tunnel. John Henry's pride was touched. "A man ain't nothin' but a man," he said. "But before I let that steam drill beat me down, I'm gonna die with the hammer in my hand." And he did. John Henry raced the newfangled contraption— and won. But he died of it.

John Henry was driving on the right side of the tunnel, and the steam drill started on the left. The conditions of the race were that they would drill for thirty-five minutes. John Henry made fourteen feet, and the steam drill "it made only nine." John Henry said, "I beat 'im but I'm dead," and he burst his heart and fell down dead. And he still had his hammer in his hand. They buried him right there in the sand beside the track, and every big engine that goes by whistles. "There lies the steel-drivin' man."

There are fifty versions of the John Henry ballad and an unknown number of John Henry hammer songs to whose rhythm workmen still drive steel into solid rock. One of them goes:

> This old hammer kill John Henry
>   Drivin' steel, drivin' steel

or

> This old hammer kill John Henry
>   Can't kill me, can't kill me.

Old Dry Frye[2]

One time there was an old man named Dry Frye. He was a preacher but all he preached for was revival collections and all the fried chicken he could eat. And one time he stayed for supper and he was eatin' fried chicken so fast he got a chicken bone stuck in his throat. Choked him to death. Well, the man of the house he was scared. "Law me!" he says. "They'll find old Dry Frye here and they'll hang me for murder sure!" So he took old Dry Frye to a house down the road a piece and propped him up against the door. Somebody went to go out the door directly old Dry Frye fell in the house. "Law me!" says the man of the house. "Hit's old Dry Frye!" (Everybody knew old Dry Frye.) "We got to get shet of him quick or we're liable to be hung for murder!"

So he took old Dry Frye and propped him up in the bresh 'side the road. And way up in the night some men come along, thought it was a highway robber layin' for 'em. So they chunked rocks at him, knocked him down, and when they seen who it was (everybody knew old Dry Frye) they thought they'd killed him, and they got scared they'd be hung for murder 'cause they'd passed several people on the road who'd a knowed who was along there that night.

Well, they took old Dry Frye and propped him up against a man's cornhouse. And that man he went out early the next mornin'; and he'd been missin' corn — so when he seen there was somebody over there at his cornhouse, he ran and got his gun. Slipped around, hollered, "Get away from there or I'll shoot!"

And when old Dry Frye never moved, he shot and Dry Frye tumbled over and hit the ground.

"Law me!" says the man. "I believe that was old Dry Frye."
(Everybody knew old Dry Frye.) "Now I've done killed him
and I'll sure get hung for murder."

So he went and saw it was him and seen how dead he was
and went to studyin' up some way to get shet of him. Well,
he throwed him in the cornhouse to hide him, and that night
he took old Dry Frye down to a baptizin' place 'side a bend in
the river where they were fixin' to have a big baptizin' the next
day, propped him up on a stump on the riverbank — over a
right deep place where the bank was pretty high — propped his
elbows on his knees and his chin on his hands. Made him look
awful natural. Left him there, went on home, and slept sound.

So early the next mornin', 'fore anybody else, a little old
feisty boy came down there foolin' around the baptizin' place.
Saw old Dry Frye, hollered, "Howdy, Mr. Frye."

Went over closer.

"Howdy, Mr. Dry Frye."

Old Dry Frye sat right on.

"I said Howdy, Dry Frye."

Old Dry Frye kept on sittin'. That boy, now he was just as
feisty as he could be. He didn't care how he spoke to nobody.

"Look-a-here, Old Dry Frye, if you don't answer me Howdy
I'm goin' to knock your elbows out from under you. —
Howdy, Mr. Frye!"

So that feisty boy he reached over and swiped old Dry Frye
a lick and over in the river the old man went, right down the
bank into that deep water, sunk clean out of sight. Then that
boy thought sure he'd drownded Dry Frye. He got scared about
bein' hung for murder, but he couldn't do nothin' about it
right then 'cause he'd seen folks comin' down the road for the
baptizin'. So he hung around and directly everybody gathered
for the baptizin', and they waited and waited for old Dry Frye

to come and preach, but he didn't come and didn't come and when they got to askin' who'd seen old Dry Frye, one man said he'd left his place right after supper, and another man said why, no, he'd not seen old Dry Frye since last meetin'. And that feisty boy he 'uld let out a giggle where he was sittin' on one of the benches in the back, and the other boys 'uld ask him what he was laughin' at but he'd just get tickled again and not tell 'em nothin'. So fin'lly the folks sung a few hymns and took up a collection. So meetin' broke and everybody went on home, and that boy he went on home, too.

Then 'way along late that night he went down and hooked old Dry Frye out of the river and put him in a sack. Got his shoulder under it and started down the road to hide him somewhere. Well, there were a couple of rogues comin' along that same night, had stole a couple of hogs and had 'em sacked up carryin' 'em on their shoulders. Them rogues came over a little rise in the road, saw that boy and they got scared, dropped their sacks and run back lickety-split and hid in the bresh. The boy he never saw the two rogues so he came on, saw them two sacks and set old Dry Frye down to see what was in the other sacks. Then he left old Dry Frye layin' there, picked up one of the hogs and went on back home.

So the two rogues they slipped out directly and when they saw the two sacks still layin' there, they picked 'em up and kept on goin'. Got in home and hung the sacks up in the meathouse. Then the next mornin' the old woman got up to cook breakfast, went out to the smokehouse to cut some meat. Ripped open one of them sacks and there hung old Dry Frye. Well, she hollered and dropped her butcher knife and she got away from there in such a hurry she tore down one side of the smokehouse, broke out two posts on the back porch, and knocked the kitchen door clean off the hinges. She was sorta scared. She hollered and squalled and the men come runnin' in their shirt-tails and fin'lly looked out in the smokehouse, saw old Dry Frye hangin' up there in the place of a hog.

"Law me!" says one of 'em. "Hit's old Dry Frye!" (Everybody knew old Dry Frye.) "We'll sure be hung for murder if we don't get shet of him some way or other."

Well, they had some wild horses in a wilderness out on the mountain. So they rounded up one of 'em, got him in the barn. Then they put an old no-'count saddle on him and an old piece of bridle, and put old Dry Frye on. Stropped his legs to the bellyband, tied his hands to the saddlehorn and pulled the reins through, stuck his old hat on his head, and then they slipped out and opened all the gates. Opened the barn door and let the horse go. He shot out of there and down the road he went with the old preacher-man a-bouncin' first one side and then the other. And them rogues run out and went to shootin' and hollerin', "He's stole our horse! Stop him! Somebody stop him yonder! Horse thief! Horse thief!"

Everybody down the road come runnin' out their houses a-shoutin' and hollerin' and a-shootin' around, but that horse had done jumped the fence and took out up the mountain and it looked like he was headed for Kentucky.

And as far as I know old Dry Frye is over there yet, a-tearin' around through the wilderness on that wild horse.

The Leprechaun[3]

Once there was a leprechaun that lived high in a tree. The tree was on the edge of a wild bright field, and behind the tree was a rich dark forest. The village people far across the field

---

[3]Jay O'Callahan, "The Leprechaun;" *The Yarnspinner,* vol. 6, no. 1 (January 1982), pp. 4–5. Reprinted by permission of the National Association for the Preservation and Perpetuation of Storytelling, Jonesborough, Tenn.

lived by the sea and stayed away from field and forest because the leprechaun lived there. The wonderful thing about the leprechaun was that he made fine shoes, but the strange thing was that he was always barefoot, for every time he made a pair of shoes he'd hear some human crying. The leprechaun would seek out the crying, give his shoes away, and the crying would stop.

Today the leprechaun lay high on a branch, wiggling his toes in the breeze. The bright spring air tingled his nose like a thousand spices.

"Tree," the leprechaun declared, "I think I'll go down to the field and see the butterflies."

"Good," said the tree in a deep serious voice that was truly rooted to the earth.

The leprechaun tumbled freely down from branch to branch, tickling the tree as he went. The village in the distance looked especially bright because the drying clothes were snapping on the lines and the fishing boats were bobbing in the sparkle of the sea.

The leprechaun swung around a last branch and jumped to the grass below. Slapping his friend the tree, the leprechaun said, "I'll be off now to romp among butterflies."

"I'll stay right here," the tree replied.

"You do that," leprechaun said, laughing politely. It was the tree's only joke. Soon the leprechaun was somersaulting in the field's high grass. He was bounding happily about among the flowers and butterflies when he cried out, "Owwwwww! A bee bit me in the toe!"

His little toe was red and throbbing and swelling up big as a strawberry.

"Bee!" he shouted. "Why'd you bite me in the toe?"

The bee buzzed nonchalantly over, "Bzzzzzzzz, wear shoes, wear shoes."

Furious, the leprechaun hopped back to his friend the tree. "Tree," the leprechaun called angrily, "what kind of shoes shall I make myself?"

"Make shoes so you can walk up my trunk, out on my branch, and enjoy yourself."

"Good!" the leprechaun said pleased. "Now I'm going down to the lake to see the bird."

"I'll stay right here," the tree said, as the leprechaun limped off.

Down at the lake the leprechaun saw his tiny friend.

"Hey bird," he called, "what kind of shoes shall I make myself?"

The bird fluttered up, saying, "Make shoes with a golden wing . . . no, two golden wings." The bird was suddenly excited. "Better still, make four golden wings. Then you could fly above and see the world as I do."

"Good!" the leprechaun squealed and left. The leprechaun climbed his friend the tree and began at once to work. He carved the shoes out of a knob of wood he kept there for the job. The moment the shoes took shape, they became as soft as the finest leather. The sun was setting when he finished the first golden wing and it fluttered alive in the dying light of day. The leprechaun was weary so the second wing took hours. The moment he finished, it burst alive like a gold flame in the dark. He could do no more; his hands and arms ached and the leprechaun lay back and fell asleep upon the branch.

He did not sleep long before the night was pierced with a human cry of pain.

"Oh," he groaned awake, "someone's crying." The shoes weren't finished so he had to climb down barefoot. Stiff and aching, the leprechaun went in search of the trouble. It didn't take him long to find it. At the far end of the forest an eight-year-old boy named Connor sat weeping by a tree. Connor was lame and could not run well, and this is his story.

Connor and the other children would arrive early at the school and the master was often late. The boys and girls would race around but Connor would pick up a stick and do the most wondrous drawings in the dusty dirt. But a ritual grew up around the drawings. The bigger boys led by a bully named Dirk would come over, stamp out Connor's drawings, and pull him to his feet. "Whyn't you be a man, Connor, and run? We're gonna have a race right now." Twenty boys would be lined up and Dirk would cry out "Go!" The race around the schoolhouse would begin, and Connor would come in a sad last. "You're so slow Connor," Dirk would sneer. Dirk's wild red face looked as if it had blown too hard on a stuck whistle. "Now we're racin' up that tree Connor. Don't be last. Go!" The climbing race would begin, and Connor would be a sad last.

Connor was bitter sick of it and tonight he sat in the dark, saying, "I know the drawings are good. They don't bother to look at them. I hate the school. I hate it!"

The leprechaun could see in the dark and, although Connor's tears were as bitter as lemon drops, the leprechaun turned his back, saying, "I cannot help the boy."

The leprechaun returned to the tree to sleep. At dawn the leprechaun woke and feverishly began to work and soon the shoes with the golden wings were finished. The leprechaun walked down the trunk of the tree and the tree cried out "Brave shoes!"

"They are," leprechaun agreed. "I'm going to show my friend the bird."

"I'll stay right here," the tree said.

The leprechaun ran down to the lake. "Hey bird, look!"

"Come," said the bird, "we'll go flying above the sea."

They flew above the field and village and now above the dazzling sea. "You live a wondrous life seein' sights like these," the leprechaun cried out.

"We all do," the bird replied. Just then there was a piercing cry of human pain.

"Oh," the leprechaun grunted angrily. "There's some trouble somewhere. I'll be back, bird." With that the leprechaun flew swiftly over the village schoolhouse.

Dirk, the huge bully, and several others had just stamped out Connor's drawing and pulled him up. Someone cried "Go!" and the race began. When Connor came in last, Dirk and two others pushed Connor into the bushes. Dirk said, "You were so slow we're gonna race around and you better not be last. And when that's done we'll race up the tree."

Connor, furious, was getting to his knees when he heard "Shhhhhh." There was the leprechaun, concealed in the bushes and looking none too pleased.

"I'm puttin' my shoes on you," the leprechaun said. The shoes stretched just right and the leprechaun laced them tight. "Now get up and race."

Connor stood up, feeling as if he were standing on the waves.

"Ready," Dirk called. "Go!" Connor flashed out ahead and flew around the schoolhouse nine times like a stallion full of life before any of them got around once. Connor stood lounging against a tree as they came panting in. "Lovely day," Connor said, staring at the sky.

"Well," Dirk said, heaving so badly he had to wait a minute to get another word out.

"Keep at it," Connor said, "you'll get faster. Don't worry."

Dirk burst angrily, "Let's race up the tree."

"I'll show you how to climb the tree," Connor said. "Watch."

With his arms folded Connor walked up the trunk of the tree, out onto the highest branch, where he did a somersault and then he floated slowly down to earth.

"Come over here!" Connor ordered. "Come over here," he said severely. "Stop your gapin'. Close your mouths. Come here. You too, Dirk, before I lose my temper!" Dirk and twenty wide-eyed boys came shyly forward as Connor picked up a stick. Connor knelt down and did a wondrous drawing of a butterfly in the dusty dirt. "Sit down," said Connor gently. "I'm gonna show you how to draw." And they all learned a thing or two that day.

Late that night with the winged shoes in hand Connor ran across the leprechaun's field and stopped at his tree. "I know you're up there, Leprechaun," Connor called. His voice was as fresh as a new spring wind. "I came across your field to give the shoes back. Thank you for the best day of my life."

"You keep the shoes," the leprechaun called down. "Keep 'em all your life. Go flying above the sea and do your wondrous drawings."

"Thank you!" Connor cried from his heart. "Thank you, Leprechaun," he called again running back across the field.

The leprechaun lay on the branch for hours and finally stretched out and said to his friend the tree, "Well . . . I guess I was meant to go barefoot on this earth."

AN ORIGINAL STORY

Students in storytelling classes at the University of Hawaii are not required to write and tell original stories, but some do when given a free choice. Here is one.

The Wart Charm

by Mari Nakamura

Kazuko had a wart upon her throat that she had been trying to get rid of for several months. Until she had reached sixteen, she had not even thought about it, but now that she was grown, it bothered her very much.

It was a small thing, and looked like a flea bite, but it lay just below the "V" on her collarbone, so that sometimes when she was not careful, it showed at the crossing point of her kimono.

"It is not a bad thing," said her grandmother, feeling her own, which was higher than Kazuko's and more apparent. "No one would ever know about it unless you drew attention to it."

But Kazuko, sensitive to it, felt it even more when her little cousins asked her what it was. Was it a mosquito bite? Kazuko told them that it was. If she had told them it was an ēbō, they would have teased her unmercifully.

She tried the chant her mother had taught her as a child, as an attempt to transfer it on to something else. She tried against the mirror, against the tree in the garden, against the red-lacquered jewelry box in her chest. At least three times a day she whispered:

Ebō ēbō usture —   Wart wart go away
Utsuttara mo doruna: Once gone, don't return
Modottara yaito sueru   If you return, I'll punish
Ebō ēbō utsure!   you with burning incense
                                     Wart wart go away!

With fervor she repeated the verse, but still it remained, an ugly spot to look down upon.

One of her friends told her that the charm worked only with people, not with things. "You must put it against someone and say the chant," her friend told her, "then the other person will get it, and you won't have to worry anymore."

This made Kazuko weep into her *futon*. She didn't want to pass her misery on to anyone else.

She wondered what she should do. Then one day, while walking home near dusk, a toad crossed her path. It gave her an idea. A toad had warts all over its body; not only on his neck, but near his ankle. If only Kazuko could transfer her wart to another part of her body!

She tried getting her foot up to her neck that night, but she could not even get it up beyond her waist. Really, it was quite hopeless. She could not get her knee up to her collarbone, either, because her breast, small as it was, got in the way. Kazuko sighed.

The next day in school, Kazuko tried to think of other parts of her body that she could transfer the ēbō to. There were not many parts of the body, she realized, that could be touched by the collarbone. Perhaps one of her fingers on the left hand would do? It wouldn't bother her too much because she hardly used them. She tried putting each one of her fingers on the ēbō by turns. No, she confessed to herself that the wart would not be comfortable on any one of her fingers.

"Kawada Kazuko!" the *sensei* slammed his ruler on the desk. Kazuko jumped.

"What is it you are doing there at your desk?"

Kazuko stood. "I was — was — ."

"She was picking at her wart!" burst her younger brother. "She always does at home."

The class laughed. Kazuko, shame-faced, looked up and met the eyes of Ichikawa Akira. He, too, was laughing. With burning cheeks, she took her seat. She saw him as she hurried out of the class later that day. He was standing in the schoolyard with some of his friends — older boys, all of them — and as she passed, they broke out into laughter.

Kazuko had reached the pit of despair. Really, there was nothing left. To be publicly singled out and put to shame was like death itself. Kazuko didn't want to return to school. But she knew that she must, or her brother would tell.

In class the next day, she looked up only when the *sensei* demanded an answer of her. She said the correct one, and felt relief when he said she could be seated. After that she took a quick glance toward where Akira sat, and found — much to her embarrassment — that he was looking at her.

"You are an unusual girl," Akira told her after school, catching up with her as she was about to leave the school-grounds. "What *were* you doing in class yesterday?"

The misery of Kazuko knew no bounds. She burst into tears.

"It is cruel of you to torment me in this manner," she said, and walked quickly so as to leave him behind.

He would not be left behind, but walked with long steps beside her breathless, almost-running ones.

"A girl is many things," he said, as to the air. "And this one will be a tired hare if she does not slow down."

Kazuko, while admitting to herself that it was the truth, refused to concede it to him. She walked all the more rapidly until at length he was forced to stop. (He laughed and watched her scurry along the path.) She was very conscious of his laughter, and his eyes on her as she ran the rest of the way home.

"Grandmother," she could not help asking that night, "did you always have an ēbō?"

"Yes," replied her grandmother. "It was given to me by a toad when I was a child."

"And Grandfather still married you?" was the incredulous question.

The next day Akira said, "Wait, I will walk home with you."

"Why should you?" retorted Kazuko, before she could hold her tongue. "I am just a silly girl, after all." But she waited.

His first words were: "Why did you run away yesterday?"

"You were laughing at me."

"And so I should," Akira replied. "You are as prickly as a chestnut. If you are so worried about your ēbō, you should try this chant."

"What is it?" Kazuko asked suspiciously.

Replied Ichikawa Akira: "Kazuko is a pretty girl."

"You no longer seem to worry about your wart," remarked Grandmother one evening, looking up from her sewing. "What has become of it?"

"It is disappearing," Kazuko said.

Grandmother looked and saw that it was the same as before.

"Where is it going?" she asked, greatly puzzled.

"Out of my head," laughed the girl.

One can't be too careful with wart-charms, thought the old woman. One could never tell how they would affect *some* people.

Annotated Bibliography

FABLES, FAIRY TALES, FOLKTALES, LEGENDS,
FANTASIES, AND CHILDREN'S STORIES
FOR STORYTELLING

Akutagawa, Ryunosuke. "Rashomon." In *Rashomon and Other Stories*. Translated by Takashi Kojima. New York: Bantam Books, 1959.

The "Rashomon" was the largest gate in Kyoto, the ancient capital of Japan. This is the story of a servant who lost his job. It relates his experiences with a ghoulish old woman at this gate. The servant learns a cruel lesson from her.

Ausubel, Nathan. "Judah, the Hammer." In *A Treasury of Jewish Folklore*. New York: Crown, 1948.

A powerful version of the origin of the festival of Channukah.

Bennett, John. "How Cats Came to Purr." In *The Pigtail of AhLee Ben Loo*. New York: Longmans, Green, 1928.

A jolly Halloween story about Sooty Will, the father of all cats, and his misadventures with a coffee mill.

Beston, Henry. "The Seller of Dreams." In *Fairy Tales.* New York: Alladin, 1952.

"What kind of dreams have you?" asked Peter. "Good, bad, true, false . . . all kinds," replied the seller of dreams. "I have even a few thrilling nightmares."

Bishop, Claire Hutchet, and Kurt Wiese. *The Five Chinese Brothers.* New York: Coward-McCann, 1938.

This favorite old Chinese tale is given dramatic treatment as retold by Ms. Bishop, with pictures by Mr. Wiese. Five identical brothers have different super powers that save them all in the end. It's great fun to delight the audience when "swallowing the sea" or having an "iron neck." The story is well sequenced and easy to follow. The climax is well timed and is followed by a brief and happy conclusion.

Bowman, James Cloyd. "Pecos Bill Becomes a Coyote." In *Pecos Bill, the Greatest Cowboy of All Time.* Chicago: Albert Whitman, 1937.

Pecos Bill, until he was a grown man, believed that he was a coyote. "Later he discovered that he was a human being and very shortly thereafter, became the greatest cowboy of all time." There are other stories in this book worth telling.

Bowman, James Cloyd. "Slue-Foot Sue Dodges the Moon." In *Pecos Bill, the Greatest Cowboy of All Time.* Chicago: Albert Whitman, 1937.

Pecos Bill and Slue-Foot Sue would have been married if she hadn't tried to ride his horse with her bustle on. A story from this collection has been recorded by Jack Lester for the American Library Association (D8–CC–26).

Chase, Richard. "Chunk o' Meat." In *Grandfather Tales.* Boston: Houghton Mifflin, 1948.

This "horror" story is strictly for fun. It has a terrific climax for any storyteller who has fun in "hamming" the dramatic. Everyone who likes to tell stories should have this in his or her repertoire for the twilight hour, Halloween, or a campfire.

Chase, Richard. "The Green Gourd." In *Grandfather Tales*. Boston: Houghton Mifflin, 1948.

One day, an old woman went to the spring after a bucket of water, and she dropped her gourd dipper and broke it. Now, she had heard that, "Was you to pull a gourd 'fore it was plumb dry-ripe, it 'uld witch ye sure."

Chase, Richard. "How Bobtail Beat the Devil." In *Grandfather Tales*. Boston: Houghton Mifflin, 1948.

The Devil tries partnership farming with Bobtail. This is one time when the Devil chose the wrong partner. Bobtail outsmarted him in every deal. In conclusion, we are told that "the Devil took his hammer and went on back where he came from and ain't been seen in that part of the country since." This is a highly amusing story.

Chase, Richard. "Mustmag." In *Grandfather Tales*. Boston: Houghton Mifflin, 1948.

Mustmag is the youngest of three sisters, and, as in the Cinderella story, her mother and older sisters treat her "awful mean." But the plot of the story is entirely different from the Cinderella plot. An entertaining story.

Chase, Richard. "Old Dry Frye." In *Grandfather Tales*. Boston: Houghton Mifflin, 1948.

A humorous yarn about Dry Frye, a preacher. All he seemed to preach for was revival collections and all the fried chicken he could eat. "And one time he stayed for supper and he was eating fried chicken so fast he got a chicken bone stuck in his throat. Choked him to death. Well, the man of the house he was scared."

The humor of this story builds as the body of Old Dry Frye continues to turn up in the most unusual places and everyone who finds him attempts to get rid of him because they're afraid people will hang them for murder. Great fun for storyteller and audience.

Chase, Richard. "Old One-Eye." In *Grandfather Tales*. Boston: Houghton Mifflin, 1948.

"One time there was a rich old lady; lived all by herself. She had a lot of money; kept it right in the house on the fireboard. . . . Now there were three rogues come into the settlement and they heard somebody telling how that old lady kept all her money on the fireboard." This is a short but interesting story about how these rogues ran with fear from a dried fish "that didn't have but one eye."

Chase, Richard. "Old Roaney." In *Grandfather Tales*. Boston: Houghton Mifflin, 1948.

The story of one of the most faithful old horses you ever heard of. "She uz a good ol mare." She came home even after her back was broken. However, you laugh at this story rather than shed tears over the faithfulness. This is one of the best of the folktales.

Chase, Richard. "Soap, Soap, Soap!" In *Grandfather Tales*. Boston: Houghton Mifflin, 1948.

This story has entertainment value for any audience. It's the story of a little boy who is sent by his mother to buy soap. He's simpleminded and soon forgets what he is sent for. Although simpleminded, he is a faithful little fellow, but his attempts to remember cause him no end of trouble. The situations that arise are not funny for him but will amuse any audience.

Chase, Richard. "Wicked John and the Devil." In *Grandfather Tales*. Boston: Houghton Mifflin, 1948.

Saint Peter visits Wicked John and says, "Once every year, I walk the earth to see if I can find any decent folks left down here, and the first man who treats me right, I always give him three wishes." Wicked John's choice causes a heap of trouble for the Devil and also causes Wicked John some grief.

Chase, Richard. "Cat 'n' Mouse." In *The Jack Tales*. Boston: Houghton Mifflin, 1943.

Jack's father sends him out into the world with a hundred dollars to see what he will do with it. Jack has many adventures. He fights varmints off for three nights to protect a mouse from a witch, and the mouse turns into a beautiful girl. But this is only the beginning of Jack's adventure. We'll say nothing further than to add that Jack's father is satisfied with his son's venture into the world. Length is good for telling.

Chase, Richard. "The Heifer Hide." In *The Jack Tales*. Boston: Houghton Mifflin, 1943.

"Well, Jack's daddy had a tract of land back in the mountains, and he decided he'd give it to the boys to work. He gave Will and Tom a good horse a-piece; didn't give Jack nothin' but a little old heifer." Jack's brothers didn't help him much, but Jack finally works it out so that he has everything and much more than any of them had in the beginning. The story tells how he used his heifer hide to gain his ends. The story wouldn't require much cutting.

Chase, Richard. "Jack and King Marock." In *The Jack Tales*. Boston: Houghton Mifflin, 1943.

Jack meets up with a stranger who says his name is King Marock. This king is a roguish kind of fellow who likes to play cards. Jack wins all the king's money.

"So King Marock told Jack he'd play one more hand and bet Jack's choice of his three girls against the whole pile. Jack said, 'All right,' and he won again. However, by the time he laid his cards down, King Marock was gone and Jack couldn't tell which-a-way he went nor nothin'."

Jack was determined to have this king's daughter as his wife and unusual things begin to happen after he begins his search for King Marock, his kingdom, and his daughters.

Chase, Richard. "Jack and the North West Wind." In *The Jack Tales*. Boston: Houghton Mifflin, 1943.

Jack's brothers, Tom and Will, and his daddy have gone off somewhere looking for work. The North West Wind commences blowing and just about freezes Jack and his mother. Jack decides that he's going to stop that North West Wind so it won't blow. Jack meets a little man on his journey who is very helpful to him. Children love this Jack story.

Chase, Richard. "Jack and the Robbers." In *The Jack Tales*. Boston: Houghton Mifflin, 1943.

The old story of the boy who leaves home because of discontent, and in his wandering he is joined by an old donkey, ox, hound dog, tomcat, and rooster. They meet robbers and are victorious in their encounter with them. The plot is old, but as told in western North Carolina in *The Jack Tales,* it is delightful.

Chase, Richard. "Jack's Hunting Trips." In *The Jack Tales*. Boston: Houghton Mifflin, 1943.

There are two of these — either one could be used separately. They are the "tall tale" hunting experience, with imagination running rampant. However, they are different enough from other yarns of the same type to be interesting.

Chase, Richard. "Old Fire Dragaman." In *The Jack Tales*. Boston: Houghton Mifflin, 1943.

[Old Fire Dragaman] com-menced spittin' balls of fire. . .

some of 'em big as pumpkins. . . . Fin'ly Jack got in close and clipped him with that sword, took his head clean off."

Chase, Richard. "Soldier Jack." In *The Jack Tales*. Boston: Houghton Mifflin, 1943.

Jack catches Death and ties him up in a sock. Death has been captured many times by man's imagination down through the ages. He always gets away one way or another. Jack releases Death, and his reason for doing so leaves the reader feeling good about it. This is one of the most delightfully told of the Jack stories. The story is short and excellent for storytelling.

Coblentz, Catherine Cate. *The Blue Cat of Castle Town*. New York: Longmans, 1949.

A charming story of a cat of Castleton, Vermont, and her efforts to find a human being who could hear her and remember the river's song, "Sing, Your Own Song."

Colum, Padraic. "The Seven Great Deeds of Ma-ui." In *Legends of Hawaii*. New Haven, Conn.: Yale University Press, 1937.

"There is no hero who is more famous than Ma-ui. In the islands of the Great Ocean, from Kahiki-mo-e to Hawaii-nei, his name and his deeds are spoken of." Of his many deeds these seven are the greatest: "How Ma-ui Won a Place for Himself in the House," "How Ma-ui Lifted Up the Sky," "How Ma-ui Fished Up the Great Island," "How Ma-ui Snared the Sun and Made Him Go More Slowly Across the Heavens," "How Ma-ui Won Fire for Men," "How Ma-ui Overcame Kuna Loa the Long Eel," and "How Ma-ui Strove to Win Immortality for Men." Each of these deeds is a story in itself, or some may be combined in telling. An excellent source for many other Hawaiian legends.

Courlander, Harold. "The Liars' Contest." In *The Hat-Shaking*

Dance and Other Tales from the Gold Coast. New York: Harcourt Brace Jovanovich, 1957.
Why Anansi eats flies, moths, and mosquitoes.

Courlander, Harold. "Reform Meeting." In *Terrapin's Pot of Sense.* New York: Holt, Rinehart and Winston, 1957.
"You got to begin charity next door. But if you want to reform, it's got to begin at home." The rhythm of the Negro storyteller is preserved in these humorous and wise Southern folktales.

Cushing, Frank Hamilton. "How the Coyote Danced with the Blackbirds." In *Zuni Folk Tales.* New York: Alfred A. Knopf, 1941.
The coyote becomes enraptured with the flight and the dance of the blackbirds. They kindly give him some of their feathers and teach him how to fly. But the Coyote's pride brings him trouble. This story is most appropriate for small children.

Cushing, Frank Hamilton. "The Serpent of the Sea." In *Zuni Folk Tales.* New York: Alfred A. Knopf, 1941.
A beautiful Indian girl, daughter of the priest-chief, loved to bathe in a sacred spring of water. The Serpent of the Sea became troubled and angry at the sacrilege. When the maiden came again to the spring, what should she behold but a beautiful little child seated amidst the waters, splashing them, cooing, and smiling. It was the Sea Serpent wearing the semblance of a child. This is the beginning of a delightful Indian legend.

De Angeli, Marguerite. *The Door in the Wall.* Garden City, N. Y.: Doubleday, 1949.
Robin is the crippled son of a great lord of medieval England. He swims the moat, gets through the door in the wall, and so saves the castle, winning even the king's recognition.

De Huff, Elizabeth W. "Poh-Tay and Wind Witch." In *Taytay's Tales*. New York: Harcourt Brace Jovanovich, 1922. Poh-Tay was a little Indian boy who lived long, long ago. While hunting rabbits one winter day for his mother, a heavy storm forced him to find shelter. He entered a strange house and found himself confronted by the ugly Wind Witch. This witch loved to eat little boys. Poh-Tay faces dangerous adventure before he is finally free of the witch.

De la Mare, Walter. "The Poor Miller's Boy and the Cat." In *Animal Stories*. New York: Scribner's, 1940.
A little black cat with the graciousness and charm of Madame D'Aulnoy's White Cat, is the good mistress of Hans, who serves her for seven years "that seem but a moment."

De la Mare, Walter. "The Riddle." In *Selected Stories for Children*. London: Faber and Faber, 1947.
"When the children were come out of the cab, they were shown into their grandmother's presence. . . . 'My dears,' she said, 'I wish to see all of you bright and gay in my house. When school is done you shall do just as you please, my dears, and there is only one thing, just one, I would have you remember.'" And in this "one thing" rests the riddle of the story. This story is odd enough to be intriguing for storytelling. It would require a little cutting.

Finger, Charles. "The Cat and the Dream Man." In *Tales from Silver Lands*. Garden City, N. Y.: Doubleday, 1924.
"You must not go away," said the cat in a soft voice, stretching out one of her paws with the cruel claws showing a little. Of all the stories in this collection of South American folktales, this is the strangest.

Finger, Charles. "The Tale of the Lazy People." In *Tales from Silver Lands*. Garden City, N. Y.: Doubleday, 1924.
One of the more humorous folktales in Charles Finger's

collection. It tells of the origin of monkeys in the forests of Columbia.

Gaer, Joseph. "The Lion and the Wily Rabbit." In *The Fables of India*. Boston: Little, Brown, 1955.

"Pride goeth before the fall." It is a story similar to "Singh Rajah and the Cunning Little Jackals" in *Tales of Laughter,* edited by Kate Douglas Wiggin and Nora Archibald Smith (Doubleday).

Geisel, Theodor Seuss. *The 500 Hats of Bartholomew Cubbins.* New York: Vanguard Press, 1938.

"In the beginning Bartholomew Cubbins didn't have five hundred hats." This is one of the best of the Dr. Seuss modern fairy tales.

Geisel, Theodor Seuss. *The King's Stilts.* New York: Random House, 1939.

One of Dr. Seuss' best. This is a story of King Bertram and the Kingdom of Benn. Tree roots serve as a dike to protect the kingdom from the onrushing sea. Birds, called Zizzards, find the roots of the trees a delicacy, so King Bertram works an army of cats to protect the trees from these birds. He works hard during the day with his cats. For relaxation in the evening, he likes to play with stilts. Old Lord Droon thinks this sport undignified for a king. He attempts to keep the king from his relaxation and trouble takes over in the Kingdom of Benn.

Geisel, Theodor Seuss. *Thidwick, the Big Hearted Moose.* New York: Random House, 1948.

Another amusing story written in verse form by Dr. Seuss. Thidwick, the moose, probably has more problems than any other moose has faced. Although in verse, the story may be told in the words of the storyteller, or it may be read or told as the author wrote it.

Ginnell, George Bird. "Scarface." In *Blackfoot Lodge Tales.* New York: Charles Scribner's Sons, 1972 (reprint of 1892 edition).

Scarface is one of the most interesting of Indian legends. It is the story of a beautiful Indian princess whom many young braves want to marry, and of a young, poor man with a scar on his face who falls in love with the maiden. The maiden refuses all of the offers of marriage, for she says, "The Sun has spoken to me. He says I may not marry; that I belong to him." When Scarface proposes marriage to the beautiful maiden, she answers, "I have refused all those rich, young men, yet now the poor one asks me and I am glad." She sends the man on a mission to the sun with the promise that she will become his wife if he completes her request. The adventures of Scarface begin.

Hawthorne, Nathaniel. "The Chimaera." In *A Wonder-Book and Tanglewood Tales.* Boston: Houghton Mifflin, 1923.

An old legend of Bellerophon and Pegasus, the flying horse, very well told. Bellerophon, after a long wait, finds the horse at the Fountain of Perene. After he tames the horse, they fight the terrible monster, the three-headed Chimaera.

Jacobs, Joseph. "The King o' the Cats." In *More English Fairy Tales.* New York: G. P. Putnam's Sons, n.d.

A deceptively simple story that, when told with skill, can be chillingly eerie.

Jacobs, Joseph. "The Legend of Knockgraften." In *Celtic Fairy Tales and More Celtic Fairy Tales.* New York: World, 1971.

This legend tells of the hunchback Lusmore, whose hump was taken from his back by the fairies when he sang with them.

Jacobs, Joseph. "The Old Witch." In *More English Fairy Tales.* New York: G. P. Putnam's Sons, n.d.

"With a willy-willy way, and a long-tailed bag, Who's stole my money, all I had?" This tale is similar to "The Long Feather Bag," in *The Fairy Bag,* edited by Kate Douglas Wiggin and Nora Archibald Smith (Doubleday).

Jacobs, Joseph. "Tom-Tit-Tot." In *English Folk and Fairy Tales.* New York: G. P. Putnam's Sons, n.d.

Another version of "Rumpelstiltskin." In this story, the king marries a girl who supposedly (so sang her mother) has a remarkable talent — she can spin flax into five skeins of yarn in one day. The truth is, the girl has a tremendous appetite and eats five overbaked pies in one day. Anyway, they both live happily for eleven months. During this time the queen is given everything her heart desires. However, in the twelfth month, the queen is led to a small room to prove to her husband that she is indeed talented and industrious (part of the bargain that was made before the marriage). Well, as might have been expected, she can't spin at all. She makes a bargain with Tom Tit Tot, a small black thing with a long, twirling tail. But, his seemingly kind gesture turns out to be a nightmare for her. This entertaining story is especially good for characterization. Not much cutting is required.

James, Grace. "Green Willow." In *Japanese Fairy Tales,* edited by Lafcadio Hearn and others. New York: Liveright, 1948.

A haunting story of love and enchantment.

Jewett, Eleanore. *Hidden Treasure of Glaston.* New York: Viking Press, 1946.

Crippled Hugh is left at Glastonbury Abbey in medieval England, but a miracle happens when he rescues Brother John from the great fire.

Krasilovsky, Phyllis. *The Cow Who Fell in the Canal.* Garden City, N. Y.: Doubleday, 1957.

A happy adventure of a cow who saw the city, especially the cheese market, and captured her own hat.

Leaf, Munro. *The Story of Ferdinand.* New York: Viking Press, 1938.

A hilarious tale of the role of a docile, yet at times ferocious bull in the destinies of certain persons in a little Spanish village.

Levin, Meyer. "The Prince." In *The Golden Mountain.* London: Jonathan Cape Ltd., 1951.

A classic legend of a prince who, because he was made entirely of precious stones, had all the virtues of all the jewels in the world.

MacManus, Seumas. "Jack and the King Who Was a Gentleman." In *In Chimney Corners.* Garden City, N. Y.: Doubleday, 1937.

True to Irish fashion, Jack tricks the king into using derogatory language ("Ye're a liar!") and wins the king's daughter and a pot of gold besides.

Macmillan, Cyrus. "The Indian Cinderella." In *Glooskap's Country and Other Indian Tales.* New York: Oxford University Press, 1956.

"And since that day, the leaves of the aspen have always trembled and they shiver in fear at the approach of Strong Wind; it matters not how softly he comes, for they are still mindful of his great power and anger because of their lies and cruelty to their sister long ago."

Mohan, Beverly, ed. "Punia and the King of the Sharks." In *Punia and the King of the Sharks.* Chicago: Follett, 1964.

A Hawaiian legend retold by Beverly Mohan. A brave and clever Hawaiian boy outwits the King of the Sharks and makes the bay and the lobster cave safe for the fishermen and the villagers. An exciting story with much action.

Parker, Arthur. "The Ghost of the Great White Stag." In
Skunny Wundy and Other Indian Tales. Garden City, N. Y.:
Doubleday, 1926.

"Timber Wolf grew cold with terror and stood as if frozen
to the ground." This story has suspense.

Parker, Arthur. "How Rock-Dweller, the Chipmunk, Gained
His Stripes." In *Skunny Wundy and Other Indian Tales.* Garden City, N. Y.: Doubleday, 1926.

We are told by this story that once upon a time, the chipmunk was a dismal clay color. The other squirrels, all gaily
colored, made fun of the chipmunk. This story tells of how
the change occurred, how the chipmunk gained his stripes.

Parker, Arthur. "The Porcupine's Quills." In *Skunny Wundy
and Other Indian Tales.* Garden City, N. Y.: Doubleday, 1926.

"Get out of my way, Gray One," growled the bear, "hurry
up, hurry up!" "I don't like to hurry," answered the Gray
One, the soft-skinned porcupine. The poor porcupine was
trampled by the bear. The bobcat and other animals all
treated the porcupine just as meanly as did the bear. Finally,
the fox offered to help the poor mistreated porcupine and we
have the story of how the animal got his quills.

Price, Edith Ballinger. "The Unhappy Echo." In *Stories
to Dramatize,* edited by Winifred Ward. New Orleans:
Anchorage Press, 1952.

A modern fairy tale that is captivating in its humor and
whimsical charm. It has great appeal for children, and for
many adults. The plot itself is unique and full of fantasy.
After all, what could be more charming than a "round, small
Echo who was quite soft and fuzzy"?

Pyle, Howard. "The Apple of Contentment." In *Pepper & Salt.*
New York: Harper and Brothers, 1913.

A different version of the Cinderella story. The youngest sister is as usual dressed in rags and has to drive the geese to the hills every morning. She is given barely enough to eat. She finds a beautiful red cap, and by her bargaining with a little old man, the owner, for something of value in exchange, she obtains an enchanted apple seed. She plants the seed by her window. The next morning a beautiful apple tree has grown with apples that only she can pick. A king comes who wants an apple from the tree and, as you would expect, the wicked mother does not want the king to know that only her youngest daughter can pick the apples.

Pyle, Howard. "Clever Peter and the Two Bottles." In *Pepper & Salt*. New York: Harper and Brothers, 1913.

"Yes, Peter is clever," so said his mother. The minister and all of the village said Peter was but a dull block. "Maybe Peter was a fool, but as the old saying goes, 'Never a fool tumbles out of a tree but he lights on his toes.' So now you shall hear how that Peter sold his two baskets of eggs for more than you or I could do, wise as we be." Howard Pyle has such a delightful style that this story could be used either for storytelling or interpretive reading.

Pyle, Howard. "Hans Hecklemann's Luck." In *Pepper & Salt*. New York: Harper and Brothers, 1913.

Hans had no luck. His wife persuades him to go to a wise old woman in the wood and talk to her about it. The old woman helps Hans to find his luck, but luck can be bad as well as good. Hans' experiences with his luck make an interesting story that can be told equally well by a girl or boy.

Pyle, Howard. "How Dame Margery Twist Saw More Than Was Good for Her." In *Pepper & Salt*. New York: Harper and Brothers, 1913.

One of the most delightful tales from *Pepper & Salt*. It concerns a "good, gossiping, chattering, old soul." Dame Twist, who lives a good life seeing fairies that other people never see. While her life is happy, it would be even happier if she could hold her tongue.

Pyle, Howard. "The Skillful Huntsman." In *Pepper & Salt*. New York: Harper and Brothers, 1913.

"Showing how a man may gain ye best bargain with ye Red One by ye help of his wife."

Pyle, Howard. "Bearskin." In *The Wonder Clock*. New York: Harper and Row, 1943.

"The stars tell me," said the wiseman, "that you shall have a daughter, and that the miller's baby, in the room yonder, shall marry her when they are old enough to think of such things." This story tells of how the king bargained to have the miller's baby killed and of the events that saved its life. As you might anticipate, the baby grows to be a strong, brave young man in a very unusual setting. After proving himself, he finally marries the king's daughter.

Pyle, Howard. "Peterkin and the Little Grey Hare." In *The Wonder Clock*. New York: Harper and Row, 1943.

A great favorite with children of all ages. Peterkin's out-witting of the giant is matched only by Molly Whuppie.

Pyle, Howard. "The Princess Golden Hair and the Great Black Raven." In *The Wonder Clock*. New York: Harper and Row, 1943.

The patient princess seeks her lover even to the house of death.

Pyle, Howard. "The Swan Maiden." In *The Wonder Clock*. New York: Harper and Row, 1943.

"As for the Swan Maiden and the Prince, they flew over the seven high mountains, the seven deep valleys, and the seven wide rivers until they came to the Prince's home again."

Pyle, Howard. "The Water of Life." In *The Wonder Clock*. New York: Harper and Row, 1943.

A story of how a faithful servant works for a young prince. The servant braves all of the adventures, and the prince attempts to claim the glory. A Wise Bird, however, feels that rewards should be given to those who deserve them. The faithful servant is finally honored. The princess whom the prince wanted for his wife will marry no other but the faithful servant.

Ransome, Arthur. "Prince Ivan, the Witch Baby and the Little Sister of the Sun." In *Old Peter's Russian Tales*. Nashville: Thomas Nelson, 1971.

"And little Prince Ivan climbed up and sat on the great black horse, and waved his hand to the old groom, and galloped away, on and on over the wide world."

Rounds, Glen. "The Whistling River." In *Ol' Paul, The Mighty Logger*. New York: Holiday House, 1949.

". . . every morning, right on the dot, at nineteen minutes after five, and every night at ten minutes past six, it r'ared up to a height of two hundred and seventy-three feet and let loose a whistle that could be heard for a distance of six hundred and three miles in any direction." A story from this collection has been recorded by Jack Lester for the American Library Association (D8-CC-259).

Sandburg, Carl. "Kiss Me." In *Rootabaga Stories*. New York: Harcourt Brace Jovanovich, 1936.

At the very end of *Rootabaga Stories* are three piquant, frolicsome tales of how the letter "X" got into the alphabet. Each is short and sheer fun for young or old. I would not say which of the three is the best. "Kiss Me" is described: "She was quick and wild, the lumber king's daughter. She had never been kissed. Neither her mother nor her father nor any sweetheart ever had a love print from her lips. Proud she was. They called her 'Kiss Me.'" The other two stories about the letter "X" are called "Pig Wisps" and "Blue Silver."

Sandburg, Carl. "Never Kick a Slipper at the Moon." In *Rootabaga Stories*. New York: Harcourt Brace Jovanovich, 1936.

"When a girl is growing up in the Rootabaga Country she learns some things to do; some things not to do."

Sandburg, Carl. "Three Boys with Jugs of Molasses and Secret Ambitions." In *Rootabaga Stories*. New York: Harcourt Brace Jovanovich, 1936.

"In the village of Liver-and-Onions if one boy goes to the grocery for a jug of molasses it is just like always. And if two boys go to the grocery for a jug of molasses together it is just like always. But if three boys go to the grocery for a jug of molasses each and all together then it is not like always at all, at all."

Sandburg concludes this clever story: "A secret ambition is a little creeper that creeps and creeps in your heart night and day, singing a little song, 'Come and find me, come and find me.' And the three boys did."

Sandburg, Carl. "The Two Skyscrapers Who Decided to Have a Child." In *Rootabaga Stories*. New York: Harcourt Brace Jovanovich, 1936.

One of the most charming of the *Rootabaga Stories*. "Two skyscrapers stood across the street in the village of Liver-and-Onions. Whether they whispered secrets to each other or whether they whispered simple things that you and I know and everybody knows, that is their secret. One thing is sure, they often were seen leaning toward each other and whispering in the night the same as mountains lean and whisper in the night."

Sandburg, Carl. "The White Horse Girl and the Blue Wind Boy." In *Rootabaga Stories*. New York: Harcourt Brace Jovanovich, 1936.

This is poetry in prose: "Of course, it happened as it had to happen, the White Horse Girl and the Blue Wind Boy met. She, straddling one of her white horses, and he wearing his strong hiking shoes in the dirt and the grass, it had to happen they should meet among the hills, and along the rivers of the west Rootabaga Country where they lived neighbors." Their meeting, however, does not have the prosaic twist of common lovers — it is fantasy. This would be delightful for a storyteller with "a touch of the poet."

Sandburg, Carl. "The Wooden Indian and the Shaghorn Buffalo." In *Rootabaga Stories*. New York: Harcourt Brace Jovanovich, 1936.

"It was past midnight. The Wooden Indian in front of the cigar store stepped down off his stand. The Shaghorn Buffalo in front of the haberdasher shop lifted his head and shook his whiskers, raised his hoofs out of his hooftracks." And what happened creates a delightful picture, depicted in a few hundred words. Fine for storytelling.

Sawyer, Ruth. "The Holy Lake." In *The Long Christmas*. New York: Viking Press, 1941.

An austere and beautiful Christmas story of a village in the Dolomites that sank beneath the waters of a lake. This is a fine Christmas story that is excellent for storytelling at any time of the year.

Sawyer, Ruth. "The Juggler of Notre Dame." In *The Way of the Storyteller*. New York: Viking Press, 1942.

"Here is an old story told by French mothers to their children for many centuries. It is as old as the market place at Cluny, old as the Abbey, and the figure of Our Lady over the doorway."

Sawyer, Ruth. "A Matter of Brogues." In *The Way of the Storyteller*. New York: Viking Press, 1942.

A miserly cobbler has his wares bewitched by a fairy song.

Sawyer, Ruth. "The Peddler of Ballaghadereen." In *The Way of the Storyteller.* New York: Viking Press, 1942.

The advice that Saint Patrick gave the peddler and what came of it is the plot. There's an appealing Irish lilt in the story.

Sawyer, Ruth. "Señora, Will You Snip? Señora, Will You Sew?" In *The Way of the Storyteller.* New York: Viking Press, 1942.

When a young girl of Sevilla is to be married, but is too poor to buy a wedding dress, she is told, "Go to the Dominican Virgin and pray to her. She will see that you have a dress and a mantilla to wear."

Scudder, Horace. "The Flying Dutchman." In *The Book of Legends.* Boston: Houghton Mifflin, 1927.

A very old legend entertainingly related by Scudder. This is the story of Diedrich, a lonely man, who was returning by ship to Holland after making his fortune. He planned on using his wealth to establish a home for the poor children of Amsterdam. One of the sailors learns of all the money the man has. He plots with other sailors to mutiny. They throw Diedrich, the captain, and the two mates into the sea. As the mutineers sail for the nearest port, a horrible plague breaks out on the ship. No port will let them land. Finally, a great storm breaks out and whenever they attempt to land they are driven out to sea — never to land. The lonely ship is said to yet be sailing the high seas.

Scudder, Horace. "The Proud King." In *The Book of Legends.* Boston: Houghton Mifflin, 1927.

A king who ruled many lands became too proud of his accomplishments for any good. One day while the king is bathing, a man who looks just like the king steals his kingly raiment. This stranger fools all of the king's followers. The real king suffers much trying to regain his kingdom. It is only after he humbles himself, saying, "Once I thought there was no one greater than I, on earth or in heaven. Now I know that I am nothing," that his kingdom is returned to him. This is one of the best of the old legends for storytelling.

Scudder, Horace. "Saint George and the Dragon." In *The Book of Legends*. Boston: Houghton Mifflin, 1927.
A very old legend well told by Scudder. "In the country of Libya in Asia Minor there was a town called Silence and near the town was a pond and this pond was the rowing place of a monster dragon. Many times had great armies been sent to slay him but never had they been able to overcome him." A Christian knight named George arrives in time to save the town of Silence and also to save the king's daughter, who was to be sacrificed to the dragon.

Shedlock, Marie. "To Your Good Health." In *The Art of the Storyteller*. New York: Dover, 1951.
"Long, long ago there lived a king who was such a mighty monarch that whenever he sneezed everyone in the whole country had to say, 'To your good health!' Everyone said it except the Shepherd with the bright blue eyes, and he would not say it."

Shephard, Esther. "The Winter of the Blue Snow." In *Paul Bunyan*. New York: Harcourt Brace Jovanovich, 1941.
"It was so cold that winter that the loggers all swore blue streaks and the snow all turned blue . . . [it] came down blue in the first place and then turned bluer after it touched the ground, too."

Thurber, James. *Many Moons*. New York: Harcourt Brace Jovanovich, 1943.
There is humor and childlike wisdom in this story of a

princess who wanted the moon.

Travers, Pamela. *Mary Poppins.* New York: Harcourt Brace Jovanovich, 1972.

There are a number of Mary Poppins books which children enjoy enormously. Some of them are: *Mary Poppins Comes Back, Mary Poppins in the Park,* and *Mary Poppins Opens the Door.* Each chapter is a complete adventure story.

Velarde, Pablita. "First Twins." In *Old Father the Storyteller.* Globe, Ariz.: Dale Stuart King, Pub., 1960.

An old couple who had beseeched the Great One for children for a long time suddenly found two baby boys on their premises. The twins grew to be no ordinary men but *Koshares* with supernatural powers. They used their powers for the good of their parents and other Indians.

Westervelt, W. D. "The Water of Life of Ka-ne." In *Legends of Old Hawaii.* Rutland, Va.: Charles E. Tuttle, 1915.

"The Hawaiians of long ago believed that somewhere along the deep sea beyond the horizons around their islands, or somewhere in the cloud-land above the heavens, there was a lake of living water which had the power to restore life. This water was called 'Ka wai ola a Ka-ne' — the water of life of Kane." Ka-ne was one of the four greatest Gods of the Polynesians in whose care the water was believed to be. Major characters are the old king, his three sons, a dwarf, and a princess. Best told by someone who can pronounce Hawaiian words.

Weston, Christine. *Bhimsa, the Dancing Bear.* New York: Charles Scribner's Sons, 1945.

The lively adventures of a boy and a performing bear in India.

Wheeler, Post. "The Little Humpbacked Horse." In *Russian Wonder Tales.* New York: Beechhurst Press, 1946.

Through the devotion and aid of the little humpbacked horse, Little Fool Ivan performs miracles and wins the beautiful Tsarita.

Woodson, Carter Godwin. "The Disobedient Daughter's Marriage." In *African Myths Together with Proverbs.* San Mateo, Calif.: Associated Pub., 1948.

Proud Afiong marries a handsome stranger only to discover that he is really nothing but a skull.

SHORT
STORIES FOR STORYTELLING

Aiken, Conrad. "Impulse." In *Short Story Masterpieces,* edited by Robert Penn Warren and Albert Erskine. New York: Dell, 1954.

A careful study of a weak, self-centered man, whose biweekly escape, staying out for the evening and playing bridge, leads him into trouble. Michael Lowes, the weakling, has been controlled by impulse most of his life. He has pulled through by the "skin of his teeth," but finally . . . ?

Asquith, Cynthia. "The Corner Shop." In *Fireside Book of Ghost Stories,* edited by Edward Wagenknecht. Indianapolis: Bobbs-Merrill, 1947.

A young attorney with a love for bric-a-brac finds mystery in a curiosity shop. Both the living and the dead meet him there. Although it is the living who first interest him, it is the dead — unknown to him as dead at the time — who influence his life the more. The ending has a surprise element.

Beaumont, Charles. "A Classic Affair." In *Night Ride and Other Journeys.* New York: Bantam Books, 1964.

A clever and interesting story with a twist that leaves you smiling. A young wife tells a former boyfriend, who still loves her, that her husband is untrue to her. She asks the young man's help to prove that her husband is unfaithful. The former boyfriend undertakes his assignment and to his amazement finds that the husband on his nights out is not seeing a woman but a beautiful custom-built car in a second-hand car lot. The husband has become enamored of this car, which is priced too high for him to buy.

The former boyfriend has a bright idea. He'll borrow money, buy the car, and give it to the husband, if he'll promise to divorce his wife. He completes his plans, but driving the car changes his life.

Beaumont, Charles. "Song for a Lady." In *Night Ride and Other Journeys.* New York: Bantam Books, 1964.

An unusual story of a newly married couple determined to spend their honeymoon on the *Lady Anne,* an old ship taking its last voyage. When they arrive for the sailing, they are astonished to learn that the passengers are opposed to their boarding. In fact some offer them money to sail on another ship. But they are determined to sail on the *Lady Anne.* Soon after leaving port they are surprised to find that the passengers are all older people who sailed years ago on the ship for their honeymoon. There is something very peculiar about their attitudes. The story is suspenseful and has a surprise ending.

Benson, E. F. "The Room in the Tower." In *Fireside Book of Ghost Stories,* edited by Edward Wagenknecht. Indianapolis: Bobbs-Merrill, 1947.

Excellent suspense is established by the relating of a dream sequence which finally is experienced in reality. The narrator dreams for years of a large house with a tower room. By the bed in this room hangs the picture of an old lady who seems to hate him. One day he is invited to a house that is a duplicate of the house in his dreams. In this house there is also the tower room, bed, and picture hanging by it. The climax is ghostly and unnerving.

Biggs, Gloria Nenstadt. "The Cat." In *19 Tales of Terror,* edited by Whit Burnett and Hallie Burnett. New York: Bantam Books, 1957.

"The Cat" is a well-written, low-key story that arrives at a very dramatic climax. It is the tale of a husband and wife who live with an underlying hatred for each other. The wife is afraid of cats; the husband ridicules her fears. He gives her a kitten as a surprise present. His expressed reason for the gift is that living with that which she fears will help her overcome her fear, yet you sense that the gift was not motivated by love and concern. The results of the gift are not what might be anticipated.

Bowen, Marjorie. "The Avenging of Ann Leete." In *Fireside Book of Ghost Stories,* edited by Edward Wagenknecht. Indianapolis: Bobbs-Merrill, 1947.

A mysterious tale comes to light through the strange connection of a portrait of a young woman in dark green, a gold medal, and a mural tablet in an old church in Scotland. There are interesting characters, predominantly male, in the story.

Bowen, Marjorie. "The Crown Derby Plate." In *Fireside Book of Ghost Stories,* edited by Edward Wagenknecht. New York: Bobbs-Merrill, 1947.

Martha Pym runs an antique business in London. One Christmas season she visits two old friends in the country. As they sit around a cozy fire chatting, Miss Pym remembers that she bought a set of Crown Derby china at an auction some thirty years earlier. It was a perfect set, with the exception of one missing plate. Miss Pym decides that she will drive to the house where the auction was held to inquire if the plate was ever found. She finds the plate, but in finding it, she has a hair-raising experience. The story has distinct personalities and the possibility of considerable dialogue.

Burrage, A. M. "The Green Scarf." In *Fireside Book of Ghost Stories,* edited by Edward Wagenknecht. Indianapolis: Bobbs-Merrill, 1947.

This story is long, but can be successfully cut. The length presents about the only problem in using this thriller for storytelling. An old castle is haunted and the ghosts return in fury. This is a natural for a storyteller with a dramatic flare.

Butter, Elvis Parker. "Pigs Is Pigs." In *Tall Short Stories,* edited by Eric Duthie. New York: Ace Books, 1959.

A humorous story about a railroad agent's misconception of the guinea pig: "Pets them animals may be, an' domestic they be, but pigs I'm blame sure they do be, an' me rule says plain as the nose on yer face."

Because this agent is determined to charge the same freight rate for guinea pigs as for any pig, he runs into trouble. Before he gets rid of the two guinea pigs that started all his trouble, he has a station full of guinea pigs. This is delightful for storytelling. "Pigs Is Pigs" can be found in many sources.

Chekhov, Anton. "An Upheaval." In *50 Great Short Stories,* edited by Wilson Crane. New York: Bantam Books, 1974.

A young girl has just finished her studies at a boarding school. She returns from a walk to the house of the Kushkins (with whom she has been living as a governess) and finds the household in a turmoil. One of Madame Kushkin's diamond brooches has disappeared. The young governess finds that her room has been searched. The story has a surprise ending; however, it is interesting primarily as a study of the emotional upheaval within the girl because the family has doubted her honesty enough to search her room.

Cochran, Robert W. "Foot of the Giant." In *19 Tales of Terror*, edited by Whit Burnett and Hallie Burnett. New York: Bantam Books, 1957.

This story holds the possibility for excellent characterization. It would not require much cutting and builds suspense that will hold an audience. This is the story of an old man whose neighbors think him odd. His story of strange happenings is convincing. You'll almost believe that he saw an unusual giant after reading the story.

Collins, Wilkie. "The Dream Woman." In *Fireside Book of Ghost Stories,* edited by Edward Wagenknecht. Indianapolis: Bobbs-Merrill, 1947.

The plot of this story is not unusual, but the character of Isaac Scotchard is arresting. Isaac's life is filled with bad luck. He marries the beautiful woman of his dreams and tragedy follows. The tale is long, but can be cut easily for storytelling.

Crane, Stephen. "The Bride Comes to Yellow Sky." In *Short Story Masterpieces,* edited by Robert Penn Warren and Albert Erskine. New York: Dell, 1954.

In the words of John Cronin, storyteller, "Creating Scratchy Wilson was particularly challenging. Being drunk is one thing, conveying a drunk is another. Jack Potter, the marshall, has to be strong and firm, yet also bashful and embarrassed. He is bringing home his bride to an unsuspecting town, never knowing the drama that will confront him. The reason I chose this story was because it truly belongs in *Short Story Masterpieces.* It is totally entertaining, tight, and precise. I can only be in awe of Crane's creativity and mastery of his craft. I may not be able to write like that yet, but I can at least tell the story for others to enjoy."

Derleth, August. "The Shereton Mirror." In *Fireside Book of Ghost Stories,* edited by Edward Wagenknecht. Indianapolis: Bobbs-Merrill, 1947.

The Pepperalls move to a small town in Wisconsin where their Aunt Hattie had lived and died. They take up residence in an old-fashioned Middle Western mansion, and live a secluded life, as they had done in New Orleans. Although dead, Aunt Hattie won't let the Pepperalls live in peace. Tragedy comes to their lives in a dramatic climactic sequence. The story is not long and follows an easy-to-remember plot.

Du Maurier, Daphne. "The Escort." In *Fireside Book of Ghost Stories,* edited by Edward Wagenknecht. Indianapolis: Bobbs-Merrill, 1947.

A sentimental ghost story that speaks of the love old English sailors have for their country. Sailors and a ship from bygone days return to escort an English ship through the North Sea during the Second World War. This is a well-written story that should challenge the storyteller who has a feel for the sea and an understanding of the first mate, William Blunt, the narrator.

Grahame, Kenneth. "The Reluctant Dragon." In *Dream Days.* New York: Dodd, Mead, 1975.

The recording by Boris Karloff (Caedmon T. C. 1974) offers a brilliant example of how this story might be told. It is an extravagant and humorous story to be told very seriously.

Marquis, Don. "The Revolt of the Oyster." In *The Best of Don Marquis.* Garden City, N. Y.: Doubleday, 1946.

A satirical story of man's first tasting of the oyster. The story needs cutting but could be extremely funny with the establishing of the appropriate mood.

Maupassant, Guy de. "The Duel." In *Selected Tales of Guy de Maupassant.* New York: Random House, 1950.

The story of a man "who cut something of a figure, as the saying is. He had an attractive form, enough readiness of speech to make some attempt at wit, a certain natural grace of manner. . . . " An interesting study of fear.

Maupassant, Guy de. "The Little Cask." In *Selected Tales of Guy de Maupassant.* New York: Random House, 1950.

One of de Maupassant's best tales for storytelling, this is the story of an old woman and an innkeeper who tries to get her plot of land, which adjoins his. It could be quite easily cut: the characters in the story are few and carefully dilineated, and the suspense, which builds to a rather unusual twist, holds.

Maupassant, Guy de. "A Strange Fancy." In *Selected Tales of Guy de Maupassant.* New York: Random House, 1950.

The story of unselfish love, of a girl's love for a boy who remains the one important force throughout her life. Although she never receives any tangible rewards for her love, she continues to love and to give to the one she loves until she dies.

Maupassant, Guy de. "Two Little Soldiers." In *Selected Tales of Guy de Maupassant.* New York: Random House, 1950.

A well-developed study of the relationship of two people — two ordinary human beings who seem to like the same things and, because of this, live for a time in perfect harmony. They meet a girl. They continue to like the same things, but with a girl entering their lives, things (as usual) change. Life becomes tragedy for one.

Northcote, Amyas. "Brickett Bottom." In *Fireside Book of Ghost Stories,* edited by Edward Wagenknecht. Indianapolis: Bobbs-Merrill, 1947.

Two sisters are taken to the country for a vacation by their father, the Reverend Arthur Maydew. They enjoy walking. One evening, Alice, the younger sister, sees in a valley a house they have never before noticed. She points it out to her older sister, Maggie. Maggie is unable to discern the house, but blames her inability to see the house on her near-sightedness. The house intrigues Alice. She leaves by herself the next day to visit it . . . and never returns, nor is she ever found. The story is well written and not so long that cutting would be a major problem.

Reid, Forrest. "Courage." In *Fireside Book of Ghost Stories,* edited by Edward Wagenknecht. Indianapolis: Bobbs-Merrill, 1947.

Michael, walking from the station to his grandfather's house, notices the high stone wall that lines one side of the long country lane. He wonders what lies beyond it. Michael's curiosity leads him beyond the wall, and the story of his experiences is one of heroism even though the things that happen to him are supernatural. This is an excellent story for telling, filled with suspense and short enough that it doesn't need much cutting.

Squier, Emma-Lindsay. "The Totem of Amarillo." In *Treasury of Cat Stories,* edited by Era Zistel. New York: Greenburg, 1944.

The story of a brave cat that lived in the Indian village of Old Man House. The ending is melodramatic but interesting. The plot can easily be recalled.

Thurber, James. "The Catbird Seat." In *50 Great Short Stories,* edited by Milton Crane. New York: Bantam Books, 1974.

Here Thurber uses the same plot he used in "The Unicorn,"
but with a different twist. Mr. Martin turns the tables on
Ulgine Barrows. She is attempting to prove him inefficient
in a job that he has held for years. In conclusion we find her
forcefully taken from her office "screaming imprecations at
Mr. Martin, tangled and contradictory imprecations."

Thurber, James. "If Grandfather Had Been Drinking at Ap-
pomatox." In *Tall Short Stories,* edited by Eric Duthie. New
York: Ace Books, 1959.

The imaginary situation has stimulated Thurber to write
some very humorous dialogue. The conclusion, "Then he
[Grant] handed his sword to the astonished Lee. 'There you
are, General,' said Grant, 'we damn near licked you. If I'd
been feeling better we would of licked you.'"

Tilden, Freeman. "The Thick Fog." In *Literature for Interpretation,* edited by Gladys Bates and Helena Kay. Boston:
Expression Co., 1941.

"The fog which had been thickening all forenoon, rolled up
the Thames estuary after midday and blotted out." An interesting, suspenseful story about a merchant who tries to find
his way home in the blackness of the fog.

Turnbull, F. G. "Ginger: An Outlaw." In *Treasury of Cat Stories,*
edited by Era Zistel. New York: Greenburg Pub., 1941.

This story of a wild cat has action and suspense. Although
Ginger is an outlaw and at times brings havoc to the Craig's
farm, his courage gains admiration. The introduction needs
cutting, but the story moves once started.

Wexler, Jerry. "I Am Edgar." In *19 Tales of Terror,* edited by
Whit Burnett and Hallie Burnett. New York: Bantam
Books, 1957.

A sophisticated terror story of a mentally ill professor who
escapes reality by finally thinking of himself as another
"Edgar." The story would have to be handled with under-

standing and sensitive interpretative insight.

Wilkin, Mary E. "The Southwest Chamber." In *Fireside Book of Ghost Stories,* edited by Edward Wagenknecht. Indianapolis: Bobbs-Merrill, 1947.

Two sisters, Sophia and Amanda Gill, inherit a house from their Aunt Harriet, who disliked them while she was living. The sisters use the house as a rooming and boarding home. Strange things happen to the guests who stay in their aunt's room. The story creates suspense and builds to a good climax, but it requires considerable cutting.

SHORT STORIES AND NOVELS FOR INTERPRETATIVE READING AND STORYTELLING

Baker, Ray Staunard. "A Ship of Souls." In *Literature for Interpretation,* edited by Gladys Bates and Helena Kay. Boston: Expression Co., 1941.

The purpose of this story is to inspire. It is a human-interest story with dramatic appeal. A convalescent in a hospital calls upon another patient, who is dying. To the visitor's surprise he finds the dying man as interested in things happening in the world as he would be if he had years to live. Finally it comes to the visitor that the dying man was living as a man ought to live, in the only moment he ever really possesses — this moment!

Benet, Stephen Vincent. *The Devil and Daniel Webster.* New York: Holt, Rinehart and Winston, 1937.

This short story has won acclaim as literature and in adaptation for stage and screen. The plot presents the struggle of a young New Englander to free himself from the Devil, to whom he traded his soul for financial success. Defended by Daniel Webster before a jury of ghosts summoned by the Devil, he is freed. The miracle is brought about by the eloquence of Webster. This is a powerful medium for a storyteller or interpretive reader with dramatic ability.

Bishop, Morris. "Professor's Office Hour." In *Literature for Interpretation,* edited by Gladys Bates and Helena Kay. Boston: Expression Co., 1941.

The poor college professor hardly gets to say a word. The mother of one of his students does the talking. Although the purpose of her visit is to help her son, after listening to the mother talk for two-and-one-half pages of story, you wonder how the poor son has a chance. The story is amusing because of personality projected through dialogue.

Bradbury, Ray. "All Summer in a Day." In *Twice Twenty-Two.* New York: Doubleday, 1966.

A poignant and shocking story about a little girl, Margot, on the planet Venus, where it rains and rains. The sun comes out only once in seven years; therefore, most of the children don't remember what the sun is like. But Margot remembers because she has been away from Earth for only three years. She yearns for the sun. What happens at school on the day the sun shines for only a few minutes may make you cry.

Connell, Richard. "Old Man's Taste." In *Literature for Interpretation,* edited by Gladys Bates and Helena Kay. Boston: Expression Co., 1941.

The Woodles are proud of their new house. Ellery, Mrs. Woodle's cousin and an absolute authority on "what-nots," arrives. Ellery has his fun changing almost everything in the house. Finally Mr. Woodles rebels and the real fun begins.

Day, Edgar. "Just As I Am." In *Literature for Interpretation,* edited by Gladys Bates and Helena Kay. Boston: Expression Co., 1941.

A clever story of a demanding husband. The wife, however, very cleverly has the last word. The technique she uses to

gain her demand will provoke a good laugh. "Just As I Am"
is about the right length, with very little need for cutting.

Dickens, Charles. "Child's Dream of a Star." In *Reprinted Pieces*.
New York: E. P. Dutton, 1970.
A beautifully written story — poetic in its conception. This
is the story of a life inspired, guided, and comforted by a star
in the heavens. It is inspirational rather than truly dramatic.

Dickens, Charles. "Christmas Dinner at the Cratchits." In
A Christmas Carol. Philadelphia: J. B. Lippincott, 1956.
This famous scene with the Cratchit family is fine for interpretative reading or storytelling if much of the language is
retained as Dickens wrote it.

Dickens, Charles. *Great Expectations*. Indianapolis: Bobbs-
Merrill, 1964.
A young blacksmith is made a gentleman through the
bounty of an unknown benefactor. Many dramatic episodes
in this novel are excellent for storytelling.

Dickens, Charles. *A Tale of Two Cities*. New York: E. P.
Dutton, 1958.
Perhaps the strongest of many dramatic episodes in this
classic novel is the scene in which Sidney Carton gives his
life upon the guillotine to save his friend.

Farr, Finis. "Mother Says No." In *Literature for Interpretation*,
edited by Gladys Bates and Helena Kay. Boston: Expression
Co., 1941.
An intriguing human-interest story of a mother and father
attempting to teach honesty to their son. The little boy
insists that a tiger is outside their house!

Forbes, Kathryn. "Mama and Uncle Elizabeth." In *Mama's
Bank Account*. New York: Harcourt Brace Jovanovich, 1968.
Dagmar, the youngest daughter, names her cat Elizabeth.

When it is discovered that Elizabeth is a tomcat, Dagmar rechristens him Uncle Elizabeth. A highly amusing scene.

Gallico, Paul. *The Snow Goose.* New York: Knopf, 1941.

"They tell the story of the Snow Goose today in London, in Dover, in the Channel Ports . . . wherever there are men gathered who saw the mighty bird soar, calm and unafraid, through the leaden death and blanketing smoke of Dunkirk and who owe their safety to the dark, twisted man and the small boat that those great black-tipped wings convoyed." The love between Phillip Rhayeder and the blond girl, Fritha, and the legend of the Snow Goose are told in Paul Gallico's strangely moving story.

Hawthorne, Nathaniel. "The Miraculous Pitcher." In *A Wonder-Book and Tanglewood Tales.* Boston: Houghton Mifflin, 1923.

A delightful story of a kindly old couple, Philenion and Baucis, who live in a beautiful valley with neighbors who are selfish and cruel. One evening two strange and unusual wayfarers stop at the old couple's place. The children of the valley had treated the wayfarers cruelly. The two old people, though very poor, treat their visitors most hospitably, giving them all the food left in their humble cottage. The next morning as the strangers depart an unusual thing happens. Where once there was a village lies a beautiful lake. The homes of the mean, selfish villagers are covered by water. The hovel in which the old couple lived has turned into a delightful marble palace.

Hyman, Mac. *No Time for Sergeants.* New York: Random House, 1954.

This is a delightfully funny book. It's the story of the experiences of a back-country boy in the service. Although most of the characters are men, the types are so distinct that girls can handle them successfully. Numerous scenes in the book are good for either storytelling or interpretative reading.

Kerr, Jean. *Please Don't Eat the Daisies.* New York: Fawcett Books Group, 1979.
A funny book containing a number of chapters that can be cut for storytelling or interpretative reading. The author has the ingenious ability of establishing a feeling of lunacy in situations that might seem normal to some or frustrating to others.

Loomis, Charles Battell. "The Gusher." In *Literature for Interpretation,* edited by Gladys Bates and Helena Kay. Boston: Expression Co., 1941.
A highly entertaining, short-short story (three and one-half pages) about a woman who likes to hear herself talk so much that she is never completely aware of what others are saying. The setting is an afternoon tea. The dialogue between the narrator and the "gusher" is clever.

McKenney, Ruth. "Hungah." In *My Sister Aileen.* New York: Harcourt Brace and Company, 1938.
Ruth studies elocution and Aileen takes piano lessons. At ages ten and eleven respectively, they give a demonstration of their acquired culture at a family reunion. Ruth presents a dramatic offering "Hun gah" (Hunger) that is truly terrific.

Patton, Frances Gray. "The Terrible Miss Dove." In *Ladies Home Journal Treasury.* New York: Simon and Schuster, 1946.
The heroine, Miss Dove, has taught geography in Cedar Grove Elementary School for thirty years. This is a wholesome schoolroom comedy, full of laughter, with maybe a tear.

Rosten, Leo Calvin. "Education of Hyman Kaplan." In *The Education of H*y*m*a*n K*a*p*l*a*n.* New York: Harcourt Brace Jovanovich, 1967.
Hyman is a student in the American Night Preparatory School for Adults, and never was there anyone more able to pull the King's English out of shape. Hyman's perpetual smile and everlasting "How Kay!" make him a most intriguing character.

Saki (H. H. Munro). "Tobermory." In *Treasury of Cat Stories,* edited by Era Zistel. New York: Greenburg Pub., 1944.
The setting is Lady Blemley's house party. Mr. Cornelius Appin, a guest with the vaguest reputation, claims that he has taught a cat the art of human speech. Mr. Appin is asked to bring Tobermory, the cat, to the drawing room. To the amazement of all, and to the embarrassment of some of the guests, Tobermory talks. The dialogue sparkles, and the situation has humor.

Schreiner, Oliver. "A Dream of Wild Bees." In *Literature for Interpretation,* edited by Gladys Bates and Helena Kay. Boston: Expression Co., 1941.
A well-written fantasy. A mother sits before a window darning: "The dreary hum of the bees and the noise of children's voices became a confused murmur in her ears, as she worked more slowly and more slowly." As she sleeps she dreams that the bees become human beings. They come individually to her and say, "Let me lay my hand upon thy side where the child sleeps. If I shall touch him he shall be as I." They offer her child many things. The author's style should be retained.

Schulman, Max. *The Many Loves of Dobie Gillis.* Garden City, N.Y.: Doubleday, 1951.
The adventures of Dobie Gillis make up a hilarious com-

mentary on campus life. One episode concerns a girl, one of Dobie's many loves, and a "Dr. Askit" quiz program broadcast. Another episode, a complete story in itself, is one in which Dobie decides that love is a fallacy. He says, "It is easier to make a beautiful girl smart than to make an ugly smart girl beautiful."

Steinbeck, John. "The White Quail." In *19 Tales of Terror,* edited by Whit Burnett and Hallie Burnett. New York: Bantam Books, 1950.

A sensitively told story of a self-centered woman, who wants a husband who would be like a garden. She finds the man she thinks is right. Their life is completely controlled by her love for the garden she creates. The man, because of his love for his wife, tries to abide by her whim. In desperation he finally kills that which his wife imagines to be symbolic of herself. The story ends with the husband sitting in utter loneliness.

Stern, Philip Van Doren. *Forever Now or Never.* New York: P. C. Duschnes, 1946.

This widely quoted and beautifully written legend tells how the Lord God in His righteous wrath at wars and man's wickedness would have blotted out the earth. The Son of God prevailed upon Him to give humankind one more chance. This He did, imposing this condition: "This time I shall let them discover the innermost secret of the universe — give them the power of tearing apart the atom. With this knowledge they must utterly destroy their world or remake it into a place of peace and plenty. It is for them to decide their destiny."

Thurber, James. "The Secret Life of Walter Mitty." In *The Golden Argosy,* edited by Charles Grayson and V. H. Cartmell. New York: Dial Press, 1947.

A humorous story of a mousy, ineffectual man who escapes his dull life through exciting daydreams. This story can be used either as an interpretative reading or for storytelling.

Thurber, James. "The Night the Bed Fell." In *American Legend,* edited by Robert Van Gelder and D. S. Van Gelder. New York: Appleton, 1946.

This story, in the vein of Thurber humor, is delightful for storytelling or interpretative reading. It concerns the night father slept in the old attic bed.

Twain, Mark (Samuel Clemens). *The Adventures of Tom Sawyer.* Berkeley: University of California Press, 1980.

Numerous scenes are excellent for either storytelling or interpretative reading. The whitewashing scene is one of the always-popular episodes — Tom uses diplomacy to get his friends to whitewash the fence and pay him for the privilege.

Twain, Mark. "By the Skin of His Teeth." In *Roughing It.* New York: Harper and Row, 1875.

While "roughing it" on horseback out in the "Wild West," one tenderfoot becomes separated from his party. He later turns up on foot and tells a hilarious tale of combat with a wild bull.

Twain, Mark. "Encounter with an Interviewer." In *Tom Sawyer Abroad. Tom Sawyer, Detective, and Other Stories, Etc., Etc.,* New York: Harper and Row, 1924.

This story shows how Mark Twain handled the "pert" young reporter from the *Daily Thunderstorm.* It has humorous, witty dialogue, as do most of Twain's works.

Warfield, Frances. "As Usual." In *Literature for Interpretation,* edited by Gladys Bates and Helena Kay. Boston: Expression Co., 1939.

Cleverly presents the inner reactions of a thirty-year-old sophisticated woman toward an eight-year-old girl. The casual conversation with the child and the woman's inner thoughts are both presented in entertaining manner. "As usual," the child wins over the adult even though at first the inner thoughts of the woman are antagonistic toward youth. Appropriate for interpretative reading or storytelling by a female.

White, E. B. "The Door." In *50 Great Short Stories,* edited by Milton Crane. New York: Bantam Books, 1952.

A subtle study of insanity that should stimulate the story-teller with a flare for the dramatic.

Wilde, Oscar. "The Happy Prince." In *The Happy Prince and Other Fairy Tales.* New York: G. P. Putnam's Sons, 1962.

The descriptive vignettes in this story are as important as the plot in creating and sustaining the mood. A beautiful tale that should appeal to most audiences.

Woolf, Virginia. "A Haunted House." In *50 Great Short Stories,* edited by Milton Crane. New York: Bantam Books, 1952.

A poetically written story of a ghostly couple that return to their home and find the joy that had once been theirs.

Index

189